ST. FRANCIS AND THE CROSS

St. Francis and the Cross

Reflections on Suffering, Weakness, and Joy

RANIERO CANTALAMESSA
CARLO MARIA MARTINI

SERVANT PUBLICATIONS
ANN ARBOR, MICHIGAN

Charis Books is an imprint of Servant Publications especially designed to serve Roman Catholics.

Servant Publications—Mission Statement

We are dedicated to publishing books that spread the gospel of Jesus Christ, help Christians to live in accordance with that gospel, promote renewal in the church, and bear witness to Christian unity.

St. Francis and the Cross was originally published under the title *Dalla Croce la Perfetta Letizia,* copyright 2001 Ancora S.r.l., Ancora Editrice, Via G.B. Niccolini, 8, I-20154 MILANO

Scriptural quotations are from the Revised Standard Version of the Bible, Catholic Edition, copyright 1965, 1966, by the Division of Christian Education of the National Council of Churches of Christ in the U.S.A. Used by permission.
C.M. Martini's texts were transcribed from recordings and were not reviewed by the author.

Quotes for most of the historical texts related to St. Francis of Assisi are taken from *St. Francis of Assisi, Writings and Early Biographies: English Omnibus of Sources for the Life of St. Francis,* Marion A. Habig, ed. (Chicago: Franciscan Herald), 1983. Used by permission of Franciscan Press.

Excerpt from *The Gift of Peace* by Joseph Cardinal Bernadin (Loyola Press, 1997) reprinted with permission of Loyola Press. To order copies of this book, call 1-800-621-1008 or visit www.loyola-press.org.

Servant Publications
P.O. Box 8617
Ann Arbor, MI 48107
www.servantpub.com

Cover design: Noah Pudgil Design Professionals

03 04 05 06 10 9 8 7 6 5 4 3 2 1

Printed in the United States of America
ISBN 1-56955-345-9

Library of Congress Cataloging-in-Publication Data

Cantalamessa, Raniero.
  [Dalla Croce la perfetta letizia. English]
  St. Francis and the Cross : reflections on suffering, weakness, and
joy / Raniero Cantalamessa, Carlo Maria Martini.
      p. cm.
Includes bibliographical references.
  ISBN 1-56955-345-9 (alk. paper)
  1. Spiritual retreats for clergy–Catholic Church. 2. Catholic
Church–Clergy–Religious life. 3. Francis, of Assisi, Saint,
1182-1226–Meditations. 4. Jesus Christ–Crucifixion–Meditations. I.
Martini, Carlo Maria, 1927- II. Title.
  BX1912.5.C3613 2003
  248.8'92–dc21

                                                            2003006667

Contents

Introduction

Often a person experiences moments in his life—either by choice or as a result of certain circumstances—when it is important for him to stop and find his bearings. At such moments, questions such as these will arise: Lord, where are you leading me? What is my goal in life? How can I be sure that the steps I am taking are the right ones?

Because of the pressure of numerous and diverse expectations, the criteria for evaluating one's own life and ministry can lose their evangelical flavor and take on a different character. For this reason, we need to stop and reflect from time to time on the uniqueness and originality of the Christian life, at the heart of which is conformity to Jesus and to Jesus crucified.

Francis of Assisi tried at all times to contemplate and imitate Jesus Christ in the humility of his incarnation and his passion, until he was so conformed to God that he was granted the gift of the stigmata. His teachings redefined in a particularly distinct way the uniqueness of the path to Christian maturity.

The essays in this book were first presented as talks at a retreat for priests called "Three Days of Spirituality," held February 14-17, 2000, in La Verna, Italy. Fully aware that the *strong* words presented there will interest many people and help sustain their Christian lives, we are making the fruit of our experience available to others.

Fr. Franco Gallivanone
Director, Istituto Sacerdotale Maria Immacolata
Milan, Italy

October 4, 2000
The Feast of St. Francis of Assisi

The Lord Has "Put a New Song in My Mouth, a Song of Praise to Our God"
Psalm 40:3

Franco Gallivanone

Franco Gallivanone is a director of the Istituto Sacerdotale Maria Immacolata in Milan, Italy. He gave this talk during the opening celebration of the "Three Days of Spirituality" at the basilica in La Verna.

> I waited patiently for the Lord;
> he inclined to me and heard my cry.
> He drew me up from the desolate pit,
> out of the miry bog,
> and set my feet upon a rock,
> making my steps secure.
> He put a new song in my mouth,
> a song of praise to our God.
> Many will see and fear,
> and put their trust in the Lord.
> Blessed is the man who makes the Lord his trust,
> who does not turn to the proud,
> to those who go astray after false gods!
>
> PSALM 40:1-4

The Lord has "put a new song in my mouth." With these words the psalmist reaches a climax in describing his experience of the freedom that the Lord has accomplished in his life—a life that had been threatened.

These words resound in an even more radical transition for us today. We have barely made the transition from one century and millennium to another—a transition that is not merely a chronological one.

God is the one who has set this transition in motion. It is occurring at a time when man finds himself totally weak and powerless. It is a transition that is rooted in something new. It is as though faith, which has existed forever, is now appearing—and only now—in its full reality; it is as though communion with the Lord is being manifested in a fresh and new way, more sincerely and more deeply than ever before.

This transition produces fruit and elicits a response. It is the new song that the psalmist recognizes as a gift freely given him. Yet it is truly part of his life. It is entirely from God, but at the same time it belongs entirely to the psalmist.

We have gathered here at La Verna with great expectation to take part in a spiritual experience. We need to ask with perseverance and equally with humility for the gift to experience—to the extent to which the Lord desires—a transition that will instill in us that living spring of a new song.

It is here on the mountain at La Verna that St. Francis of

Assisi—who sang the praises of the Almighty God throughout his life—experienced a fundamental transition in his life. Even though he was afflicted by illness, blindness, and trials, he experienced the gift of a new song. Now we need to ascend the mountain with him, so that we can dwell in the presence of God before descending the mountain once again to our everyday lives.

Seeking the Lord in Times of Trial

As we make our way up the mountain, it is good to remember that Francis did not climb the mountain at La Verna during a time of peace, tranquility, and solace in his life.

From the very moment of his conversion, Francis had searched for a model that might cultivate and shape his natural inclination to song. He found that model right away in Jesus—in the beauty of Jesus' life as recounted in the Gospel and especially in the shining new song of Jesus' death on the cross.

Francis became Jesus' disciple. Every step he took was characterized by a passionate desire to insure that every fiber of his being was progressively in harmony with the humanity of the Son of God, who offered himself up completely for us. Thus Francis prayed: "May the power of your love, O Lord, fiery and sweet as honey, wean my heart from all that is under heaven, so that I may die for love of your love, you who were so good as to die for love of my love."[1] This became his journey in life—a journey that was constantly confirmed and in which he continually received consolation.

Francis' preaching and ministry touched the hearts of people and brought about conversion and reconciliation. His radical way of following the Lord increasingly became a home where many brothers and sisters felt welcome. In Francis' personal journey, they encountered a radical and meaningful way of interpreting and living the gospel in the new season of history that was approaching.

Nevertheless, when Francis arrived at La Verna, the song that had been flowing seemed to have died out. He was facing a terrible crisis. The movement he had founded was becoming institutionalized and was losing its evangelical intensity. Some questioned whether such a lifestyle was totally viable.

All this had repercussions for Francis' own faith. He had begun to question the authenticity of everything that he had experienced so deeply. He doubted the divine origin of the plan he had for his life. These questions and doubts resounded amid an oppressive silence on God's part. God no longer seemed to speak to him, despite his persistence in seeking God.

Francis felt abandoned by God. He withdrew from his brothers. He did not want them to see him, since his countenance lacked its customary serenity.

Thus God's gift to Francis of a new song did not come during a time of personal peace and consolation. Rather God gave him the song at a time when—as the psalmist says—"foundations [were being] destroyed" (Ps 11:3) and everything seemed uncertain.

Questions for Reflection

What do I discover in my heart as I go up the mountain? What questions emerge from my experience of ministry, from the life of my community, from being immersed in all that is happening around me—and that I carry with me along the way? What effects does all this have on my faith?

Resistance and the Gift of a New Communion

When Francis was on the mountain, he waited upon God, not seeking consolation in anything else. He endured a terrible emptiness patiently as he waited for God to intervene.

The Lord did intervene on the mountain, but he did not

answer Francis' questions. Instead he gave Francis a new depth of communion with him. He conformed Francis to his death in a way that Francis had never experienced before. From then on, God continually showed Francis the way to enter more deeply into his paschal mystery.

This new song did not flow from Francis' openness to the Lord, nor did it flow from the almost *natural* joy that usually characterized him. Rather, God freely gave it to him because Francis had submitted himself to a radical purification. He had waited and waited patiently until he was stripped of all his human resources. At that point Francis was truly poor, and the Lord was able to dwell within him completely.

The Lord gave Francis his life. His heart and his body attained the "life of the Gospel."[2] St. Paul's words to us, which were at the center of the apostle's life and ministry, became a reality in Francis' life: "I have been crucified with Christ; it is no longer I who live, but Christ who lives in me" (Gal 2:20). Indeed, the gift of the stigmata (which Francis kept secret) was the sign of this transition.

Questions for Reflection

What do I want to ask of the Lord at this time? How do I wish to encounter him now?

Descending the Mountain in "Perfect Joy"

When Francis came down from the mountain, he looked at the world from the Lord's cross. The world, the life of the Church, his brothers, the conflicts between the city-states, and even the daily struggles that are characteristic of nature had not come to an end. But now they were enveloped in the light of the Lord's Passover, through which all of creation is called to pass as through the tiring labor of childbirth.

Francis came down from the mountain singing the new song that the Lord had put on his lips. It was the song of tenderness that he displayed toward Friar Leo, who was plagued by temptation and for whom he wrote the "Praises of the Almighty God" and the "Blessing." It was the song of praise to God that continued to flow from La Verna and exploded into "The Canticle of the Creatures." It was the song of his preaching ministry as he traveled through Umbria and through the Marches. It was the song of "perfect joy" that was not scandalized by difficulties, rejection, or tribulation but persevered in a climate of praise.

Finally, it was the song of the new concern that Francis had for his brothers. He knew that the crucified and risen Lord was the one who was looking after them with passion and might. Christ had been doing this long before Francis did and better than he could. Francis knew that he was not called to resolve everyone's problems. Rather, he was to be a sign to everyone by freely giving himself to others in faithfulness, power, patience, diligence, and mercy.

Questions for Reflection

Do I truly want the Lord to allow me to enter into the mystery of his death so I can experience the power of his resurrection? Am I asking him for the grace of a new song?

The Song Is Still New

I have one final thought concerning our bishop, Cardinal Carlo Maria Martini, whom we honor and thank in a special way on the twentieth anniversary of his service to our Church. For twenty years, in his life and in his words, he has exhorted the people of our diocese to be pilgrims on the road of the gospel. In gratitude for his ministry—a song that continues to be new after twenty years—we added the following words from one of his pastoral letters to our retreat guide for daily prayer:

> How beautiful it is to seek in history the signs of Trinitarian love; how beautiful it is to follow Jesus and to love his Church; how beautiful it is to see the world and our life in the light of the cross; how beautiful it is to give up our lives for our brothers and sisters![3]

My wish for you brother priests is that the following days will help you to experience praise—in fact, to dwell in a climate of praise. May the presence of the Lord, the help of Francis, the Word that we will hear and celebrate, the warmth and fraternity among us, help us to enter fully into the world of faith. There we will perceive a new song springing forth within us today, for the Church and for the world.

Let us continue to glorify God with that song of praise forever.

Praises of God Most High
Francis of Assisi

You are holy, Lord, the only God,
    And your deeds are wonderful.
You are strong.
    You are great.
    You are the Most High.
    You are almighty.
    You, holy Father, are
    King of heaven and earth.
You are Three and One,
  Lord, God, all good.
You are Good, all Good, supreme Good,
  Lord God, living and true.
You are love,
    You are wisdom,
    You are humility,
    You are endurance,
    You are rest,
    You are peace,
    You are joy and gladness.
    You are justice and moderation.
    You are all our riches,
    And you suffice for us.

You are beauty.

    You are gentleness.

    You are our protector,

    You are our guardian and defender,

    You are courage,

    You are our haven and our hope.

You are our faith, our great consolation.

You are our eternal life,

Great and wonderful Lord,

God almighty,

Merciful Savior.[4]

The Canticle of the Creatures
(also called "The Canticle of the Sun")
Francis of Assisi

Most high, all-powerful, all good Lord!
    All praise is yours, all glory, all honor,
    And all blessing.
To you alone, Most High, do they belong.
    No mortal lips are worthy
    To pronounce your name.
All praise be yours, my Lord, through all
    that you have made,
    And first my lord Brother Sun,
    Who brings the day; and light you give to us
    through him.
How beautiful is he, how radiant in all his splendor!
    Of you, Most High, he bears the likeness.

Praised be my Lord for our sister the Moon,
    and for the stars,
    which he has set clear and lovely in the heaven.

All praise be yours, my Lord, through Brother Wind and Air,
    And fair and stormy, all the weather's moods,
    By which you cherish all that you have made.

All praise be yours, my Lord, through Sister Water,
 So useful, lowly, precious, and pure.
All praise be yours, my Lord, through Brother Fire,
 Through whom you brighten up the night.
 How beautiful is he, how gay, full of power and strength.
All praise be yours, my Lord,
 Through those who grant pardon for love of you;
 Through those who endure sickness and trial.
Happy those who endure in peace;
 By you, Most High, they will be crowned.

All praise be yours, my Lord, through Sister Death,
 From whose embrace no mortal can escape.
Woe to those who die in mortal sin!
 Happy those She finds doing your will!
The second death can do no harm to them.

Praise and bless my Lord, and give him thanks,
 And serve him with great humility.[5]

"All Praise Be Yours, My Lord, Through All That You Have Made"

Francis of Assisi's Experience of Beauty and the Paschal Mystery

Raniero Cantalamessa

Fr. Raniero Cantalamessa is a member of the Capuchin Fathers, a Franciscan order. He is a preacher to the papal household. This meditation was given at the Monastery of La Verna on the morning of February 15, 2000.

Most people are familiar with St. Francis' "Canticle of the Creatures," but few people know the circumstances under which it was conceived. A Franciscan source document, *The Legend of Perugia*, describes these circumstances in detail:

> During his stay at this friary, for fifty days and more, blessed Francis could not bear the light of the sun during the day or the light of the fire at night. He constantly remained in darkness inside the house in his cell. His eyes caused him so much pain that he could neither lie down nor sleep, so to speak, which was very bad for his eyes and for his health.... One night, as he was thinking of all the tribulations which he was enduring, he felt

sorry for himself and said interiorly: "Lord, help me in my infirmities so that I may have the strength to bear them patiently!"[1]

This was Francis' Gethsemane, so it is no surprise that he would pray the same prayer as Jesus: "Let this chalice pass from me" (see Mark 14:36).

At this point *The Legend of Perugia* describes a vision in which the Lord gave Francis the assurance of his eternal reward. It was so consoling that Francis shared it with his fellow friars when he woke up in the morning. From it came a new resolve:

"Therefore, for his glory, for my consolation, and the edification of my neighbor, I wish to compose a new 'Praises of the Lord,' for his creatures. These creatures minister to our needs every day; without them we could not live; and through them the human race greatly offends the Creator. Every day we fail to appreciate so great a blessing by not praising as we should the Creator and dispenser of all these gifts." He sat down, concentrated a minute, then cried out: "Most high, all-powerful, and good Lord ..."[2]

The adjective that occurs most frequently in Francis' "Canticle of the Creatures" is *beautiful* or its more poetic equivalent, *fair.* He describes "Brother Sun" as beautiful; "Sister Moon and Stars" are precious and fair; "Brother Fire" is also beautiful. What is most extraordinary is the fact that Francis discovered the beauty of these creatures when he could no longer either see them or enjoy them and when even light caused him indescribable suffering.

He was at the point of being crucified both inside and out. Violaine's words in Paul Claudel's play *The Tidings Brought to Mary* could very well be his own words: "Now I am completely broken, and you can smell the sweet fragrance!"[3] In Francis' case it was the sweet fragrance of poetry besides that of sanctity.

This event from Francis' life points us in the right direction for reflecting, as priests, on the mystery of beauty. We might say the same thing about beauty that St. Augustine said about time: "What then is time? If no one asks me, I know; if I want to explain it to someone who does ask me, I do not know."[4] However, I do not intend to reflect on beauty from an *essential* viewpoint (about what is beauty and its relationship to truth and goodness) but from an *existential* viewpoint. In other words, I would like to reflect on our own experience of beauty.

Furthermore, I would like to emphasize one very precise and limited aspect of our experience of beauty. It closely concerns each one of us and is related not only to aesthetics but also to morality. It is not the beauty of the mountains and the seas; it is the beauty of the human body—especially of a woman's body. It is this beauty that generates *eros*, one of the major forces at work in the world, if not the most powerful of them all. The beauty of the mountains and seas is not erotic beauty, but a woman's beauty, together with all that it involves of which we are well aware, is erotic beauty.

This type of beauty is what people seem to be seeking most as we are making the transition to a new millennium. It has become the greatest "cult object" of our welfare society. One only has to look at the fashion world, those notorious calendars of nude women, and the roles that are assigned to women in almost every movie and advertisement.

This is a new challenge for believers. Does Christianity have something to say about this problem of beauty? Or are we condemned to repeating sterile warnings that are rooted in a certain moralistic preaching from the past?

Recently some people with authority have addressed this problem. In his *Letter to Artists* Pope John Paul II had some profound things to say about beauty, reflecting the relationship of beauty to art and to the sacred. Cardinal Carlo Maria Martini has written a pastoral letter on this topic called *Which Beauty Will Save the World?*

For priests, this is not merely a *pastoral* problem (like proclaiming the gospel in a culture that is obsessed by the problem of beauty). It is, above all, a personal problem and an *existential* problem. As Claudel wrote in one of his plays: "Man is a proud being. The only way of making him understand his neighbor was by having his neighbor become flesh. The only way he could understand dependence, necessity, and need was by being subject to the law of this different being, a law that was due to the mere fact that he exists."[5]

All men and women are subject to this law in different ways, whether they are married or single or remain celibate for the kingdom of God. For this reason it is important to clarify this point.

Many people are well acquainted with and even repeat the words that Dostoevski put on the lips of one of his favorite characters, the Idiot: "Beauty will save the world." They are also well acquainted and often repeat the question that immediately follows this statement: "What sort of beauty will save the world?"[6] It is clear that not all beauty will save the world; there is a beauty that can save the world and a beauty that can ruin it. This is the crux of the problem.

The Ambiguity of Beauty

We find one clear sign of the ambiguity of beauty within our human experience. In our modern culture, not only are there people who exalt beauty; there are others who explicitly reject it. This rejection of beauty amounts to such an "affront to beauty" that we could speak about the death of beauty, just as people speak about the death of God.

Those who have portrayed beauty in the past were almost exclusively men. Thus it's not surprising that the modern disdain for beauty translated into a disdain for women:

But, woman, mass of entrails ...[7]

While I'm the galley-slave kept chained
Down in the darkness of your breast,
While I'm the gambler in your spell,
The drunkard with the fiery thirst,
The corpse bedecked with vermin. Cursed.
I damn you to the fires of hell![8]

The artist Bernard Buffet depicts in one of his paintings monstrous birds that fling themselves on the nude body of a woman as though she were a carcass. One writer has described some of the famous women portrayed in abstract paintings as "corpses of beauty."[9]

These artistic expressions of beauty end up *demystifying* beauty and being an affront to beauty (and not only to the beauty of women). Rimbaud's words at the beginning of his collection of poems, *A Season in Hell*, are noteworthy in this respect: "One evening I took beauty upon my lap. I found her harsh, and reviled her."

In the art world, artists express this affront by provocatively portraying *vile* objects such as urinals. And in the world of literature, writers delight in the gratuitous use of obscenities.

"God," Evdokimov wrote, "is not the only one who 'clothes himself in Beauty.' Evil imitates God in this respect and thus makes beauty a profoundly ambiguous quality.... Beauty exercises its charms, converts the human soul to its idolatrous worship, and usurps the place of the Absolute. Beauty is able to accomplish this transformation with a strange and total indifference toward Goodness and Truth.... But here is the paradox: even though truth is always beautiful, beauty is not always truth."[10]

Not Sin Alone

What causes such ambiguity? What diverted us in the first place from following the light that should be guiding us on the road to happiness?

The traditional response has been sin. Yet we see in Scripture that the ambiguity of beauty was not only the effect of sin but also its cause. The very beauty of the forbidden fruit seduced Eve. She saw that the tree was "a delight to the eyes, and ... to be desired to make one wise" (Gn 3:6). Man would not have been separated from God if he had not been attracted by his creation. Of the two elements that make up sin—*aversio a Deo* and *conversio ad creaturas* (aversion to God and conversion to his creatures)—the second precedes the first psychologically.

Therefore, a deeper cause of the ambiguity of evil precedes sin itself. In fact, the ambiguity of beauty is rooted in man's very nature. He is made up of both a material and an immaterial element, of something that draws him to multiplicity and something that aspires, on the other hand, to unity.

There is no need to believe (as Gnostics, Manicheans, and so many others have believed) that these two elements can be traced back to two rival *creatures*, one that is good and created the soul and one that is bad and created the body and other matter. The same God created both one and the other in profound, *substantial* unity.

However, these elements are not static: Man cannot remain peacefully balanced between them, as if these forces had a neutralizing effect on each other. On the contrary, by concretely exercising his freedom, and guided by God's word, man himself decides in what direction he will aspire: either *upward*, toward that which is *above* him, or *downward*, toward that which is *below* him. He aspires toward unity or toward multiplicity.

Man's dignity resides precisely in this possibility of determining his own fate. Here his freedom of conscience finds a special training ground. By creating man free, writes a

Renaissance philosopher, it is as though God were telling him:

> I have placed thee at the center of the world, that from
> there thou mayest more conveniently look around and
> see whatsoever is in the world. Neither heavenly nor
> earthly, neither mortal nor immortal have We made thee.
> Thou, like a judge appointed for being honorable, art
> the molder and maker of thyself; thou mayest sculpt thy-
> self into whatever shape thou dost prefer. Thou canst
> grow downward into the lower natures which are brutes.
> Thou canst again grow upward from thy soul's reason
> into the highest natures which are divine.[11]

This explains the struggle between the flesh and the spirit.
It is why our existence in the world and our relationship with
beauty are so dramatic in nature. We face a choice.

Fragmented Beauty

During the earthquake that shook Assisi a few years ago, a
fresco by Cimabue on a vault of the upper basilica was reduced
to thousands of miniscule colored fragments. Currently
experts are trying to reconstruct the original fresco.

This destruction is an apt image of what has happened in

the transition from the uncreated beauty of God to the multiplicity of beautiful things of the world. The beauty that we experience in this life is *fragmentary*. Artistic masterpieces—works that are by definition complete, perfect, and irreproducible—are really only fragments of beauty that demonstrate its variety.

Moreover, theirs is only a transient beauty. (This is true of the living beauty of the human body, which flourishes and then decays into nothing, as well as of artistic beauty.) Although it is possible to repair the damage of a few centuries through restoration, what will remain, after a couple millennia, of all the beauty that we have created? We are fooling ourselves if we say that an artist has *immortalized* something in a painting or in a statue.

What happened to Cimabue's fresco is, at the same time, a reminder of man's obligation with regard to beauty: to rise above the fragments to the whole. Our collision course with beauty begins when we forget the whole and cling to the fragments. Returning to our original example, if someone finds a fragment of the fresco and steals it or destroys it instead of using it to restore the original fresco, he is damaging the entire project.

Using Pico della Mirandola's terminology, when do human beings "grow downward" and debase themselves in respect to beauty? Certainly not when they admire, enjoy, or create beautiful things. Rather they do so when they abandon themselves to them, when they do not use them as a springboard to incorruptible beauty through praise and desire but instead throw themselves headlong into them, making their momentary pleasure an end in itself.

St. Augustine, in a text that Cardinal Carlos Maria Martini quotes in his pastoral letter on beauty, described his experience in this regard. We can recognize our own experience in it:

Too late have I loved you, O Beauty so ancient and so new, too late have I loved you! Behold, you were within me, while I was outside; it was there that I sought you, and, a deformed creature, rushed headlong upon these things of beauty which you have made. You were with me, but I was not with you. They kept me far from you, those fair things which, if they were not in you, would not exist at all.[12]

Beauty Idolized

Created beauty can enslave human beings and thus become a deathtrap for them instead of a training ground for their freedom to choose. It is like drugs: No single dose will satisfy the need once and for all; new and stronger doses are needed to produce the same effect. And in order to appropriate and enjoy this beauty, a man does the same thing that he does to obtain drugs: He fights and he kills, or he is killed.

When judging crimes of passion, allowances are made for extenuating circumstances precisely because people recognize that the perpetrator is acting with a reduced freedom to choose. Truly, therefore, a certain disordered love of beauty *debases* man because it deprives him of that which makes him *human*—reason and the freedom to choose.

Literature offers us some well-known symbols of the two types of feminine beauty, one that is uplifting and one that leads to destruction: Dante's Beatrice and Homer's Elena. The most noteworthy example in modern days is that of Marilyn Monroe, whom polls indicate to be the modern myth of the feminine mystique that most resists time. (Sources are careful, though, not to recall how this myth ended.)

There are even some memorable cases of this ambiguity of beauty in the Bible. On one hand, we see the beauty of two lovers who try to outdo each other in admiration in the Canticle of Canticles (which we assume to be a symbol of higher spiritual realities). On the other hand, there is the beauty of the woman who dragged David into a life of adultery and crime (see 2 Sm 11:2). And Daniel said to one of the two elders who wanted to execute the chaste Susanna, "Beauty has deceived you" (Dn 13:56).

From a spiritual perspective, the Bible views such a fixation on created beauty as the very essence of idolatry, since it substitutes the creature for the Creator:

> For all men who were ignorant of God were foolish by nature; and they were unable from the good things that are seen to know him who exists, nor did they recognize the craftsman while paying heed to his works.... If through delight in the beauty of these things men assumed them to be gods, let them know how much better than these is their Lord, for the author of beauty created them.
>
> Wisdom 13:1, 3; (see also Romans 1:19-23)

This fall from a level of spiritual beauty to that of material beauty is often repeated within the creature itself, particularly women. A portrayal of feminine beauty does not usually focus on a woman's face, where her inner beauty, feelings, and thoughts—the soul of a woman—are manifested most clearly, but on other parts of her body—and always the same parts at that.

Art scholars tell us that in sacred icons the body serves as a support for the subject's face, and the face forms a frame for the subject's gaze. What we see in modern art is just the opposite: The face often serves as a pretext for depicting some other part of the female body.

There are no longer any *Mona Lisas* in the art world, and at the rate we are going, we may even lose the prospect of having any in the future. Feminine beauty has been reduced to mere *sex appeal*, a serious insult to women because people end up viewing women only in their function to men—as objects and not as subjects.

How Christ Redeemed Beauty

St. Paul wrote: "For the creation was subjected to futility, not of its own will but by the will of him who subjected it in hope; because the creation itself will be set free from its bondage to decay and obtain the glorious liberty of the children of God" (Rom 8:20-21).

In place of *creation* we can substitute the word *beauty* without altering the meaning of St. Paul's statement: "Beauty was subjected to futility [in hope of being] set free." To save the world, beauty itself first needs to be saved. In fact, Christ's work of redemption even extended to beauty, and we will see how this happened.

The contrast between two assertions about Jesus Christ is striking. On one hand, Scripture tells us that he is "the fairest of the sons of men" (Ps 45:2). On the other hand, during his passion Scripture applies the words of the poem of the Servant of YHWH to him: "He had no form or comeliness that we should look at him, and no beauty that we should desire him..., as one from whom men hide their faces" (Is 53:2-3).

Jesus redeemed beauty by depriving himself of any beauty. He did this out of love. In order to understand this paradox, we need to refer to a fundamental principle that St. Paul formulated at the beginning of his letter to the Corinthians: "For since, in the wisdom of God, the world did not know God through wisdom, it pleased God through the folly of what we preach to save those who believe" (1 Cor 1:21).

This is what Luther called redeeming things "through their opposite" *(sub contraria specie)*. When applied to beauty, it means that since man was not capable of elevating himself to the beauty of the Creator through the beauty of his creatures, God used a different method. He decided to reveal his beauty through the shame and the ugliness of his cross and suffering. From then on, beauty would be attained through the paschal mystery of death and resurrection.

This is what the example of St. Francis clearly highlights. Cardinal Carlo Maria Martini reached the same conclusion in his pastoral letter on beauty: Beauty is love that has been crucified and that has been resurrected.

The model and source for redeemed beauty is what shines on the face of Christ (see 2 Cor 4:6). Beauty is no longer "the splendor of truth" as Plato defined it but the splendor of Christ. (In reality the splendor of truth and the splendor of

Christ coincide, because Christ himself is Truth.)

From the beginning of Christianity there has been a tradition that says that God, in whose image man was created (see Gn 1:27), was not the invisible and incorruptible God. (How can man, who is made of flesh, be in the image of God, who is spirit?) The God in whose image man was created was Christ, the Word Incarnate and future man. Christ is the true and perfect Image of God (see Col 1:15); we are the image of the Image of God.[13] The degree of our beauty and perfection depends on the degree to which we resemble Christ.

The Sacrament of Beauty

This ideal of beauty has fostered Christian art and spirituality for many centuries, both in the West and in the East. Beauty has always been such an important component of the Christian outlook that there is a whole current in Orthodox spirituality that is called *filocalia*—love of what is beautiful. St. Augustine says that philosophy and *filocalia* are more than twin sisters: They are the same thing.[14]

Dostoevski tried to depict an ideal of beauty that was composed of sheer goodness and a positive outlook in his Idiot. He was not completely successful. He excused himself to those who noted this failure: "For the world there exists only one being that is absolutely beautiful—Christ, but the appearance of this infinitely beautiful being is certainly an infinite miracle."[15]

Iconographers know that the light they need to portray in their icons is not just any light but the light of Mount Tabor—the light that shone in anticipation of the Resurrection. On Mount Tabor the disciples were overwhelmed by this sense of beauty, and Peter exclaimed, "Master, it is well that we are here!" (Mk 9:5).

What is the difference between this beauty and every other type of beauty, even though here we are only examining corporal beauty? This is a beauty that comes from within and for which the body is the means of expression and not the ultimate source. The difference between this beauty and exterior beauty—which is merely composed of beautiful shapes and harmony of colors—is the same as the difference between a stained-glass window of a cathedral seen from the road and that same stained-glass window seen from inside with light shining through it. The human body becomes the *sacrament* of beauty—its sign, its expression, its manifestation, its transparency—but not its ultimate source. The body is not an opaque filter on which light is falling but rather a stained-glass window that lets the light shine through it.

Occasionally we catch a glimpse of this mystery on the faces of contemplative monks and nuns. A person might see nothing more than the face and eyes that are cast down. Nevertheless, one walks out of such a meeting and exclaims, "What faces! What light! What beauty!" The words that Claudel used in one of his plays to describe a little girl apply to these contemplatives: "Other people's eyes absorb light; yours radiate it."[16] We see this beauty on the faces of little children (at least those who have had the good fortune of growing up in a healthy environment) because it emanates from innocence and purity of heart.

Our Part in the Redemption of Beauty

Christ, therefore, has redeemed beauty through his paschal mystery, in which he let himself be stripped of every beauty. He proclaimed that the beauty of love is higher than the love of beauty itself. What does all this mean for us? Does it mean that we have to give up our quest for created beauty as well as our delight in created beauty—especially beauty connected with the human body—as we await the transfiguration of our bodies at the final resurrection?

No, it does not. Created beauty was made to embellish this life and not our future life, which will have a beauty of its own. We only need to let our quest for beauty be filtered by the cross that redeems it.

This cross of beauty is none other than love and all that it implies: being faithful to the choice that a person has made in life, whether it be matrimony or the consecrated life; respecting other people; sacrificing; and obeying God and respecting the purpose for which he made things.

Embracing the Cross

Redemption of beauty passes through an *ascesis* (discipline). This entails the practice of penance, mortification, and self-denial to promote greater self-mastery. We foster the way of perfection by embracing the way of the cross.

In the particular case of beauty, redemption involves an *ascesis* of the eyes. Feuerbach said, "A man is what he eats." In the civilization in which we now live, where images are so important, perhaps we should say, "Man is what he sees."

There is a story about a saintly monk who, having seen feminine beauty in its total splendor one day, cried out with joy and began to praise the Creator. Relating this incident in his *Ladder of Divine Ascent*, St. John Climacus commented: "He has already risen to immortality before the general resurrection."[17] We will cross this finishing line at the final resurrection.

In the meantime, it is worth recalling Job's words: "I have made a covenant with my eyes; how then could I look upon a virgin?" (Job 31:1). Those of us who are priests (and laymen as well) cannot make women bear the weight of men's struggles and shoulder the responsibility for their fall, as we often did in the past.

We thundered from the pulpit against "women's immodesty" and wrote treatises "against women's jewelry and finery."[18] We were walking in Adam's footsteps, placing the blame on God himself: "The woman whom thou gavest to be with me, she gave me fruit of the tree, and I ate" (Gn 3:12). Such an attitude has never proven to be effective and might even be downright counterproductive. We ought to confront the struggle in the same way as our sisters do from their end.

St. Augustine was humble enough to reveal his struggle in this regard, not when he was a young man but when he was a bishop. He referred, first of all, to the innumerable ways in which men make enticing what they produce—be it clothing, wares, pictures, or sculptures. Nonetheless, he praises God because he is convinced that the beautiful pictures that an artist produces, even if the purpose for which they were created is somewhat muddled, come from the One who is infinite beauty. Therefore, it follows:

I say these things and see their truth, yet I too entangle my steps in such outward beauties.... For I am caught most wretchedly, and you mercifully pluck me out. Sometimes I feel nothing, because I had not fallen deep into those snares; sometimes it is with pain, because I was already caught firmly therein.[19]

I do not know what Augustine would say if he were living today and saw our movies, television, and now the Internet. If we do not impose some rigorous choices on ourselves, all these things can end up being a cancerous growth for us, whether we are married or celibate.

Contemplating the Source

However, opening up our eyes to real beauty is much more important than closing our eyes to fake beauty. Let us contemplate the crucified and resurrected Christ in his Word, in the Eucharist, and in icons. In him beauty has been once and for all "set free from its bondage to decay" (Rom 8:21).

"A chaste man," St. John Climicus wrote, "is someone who has driven out bodily love by means of divine love, who has used heavenly fire to quench the fires of the flesh."[20] Such a man overcomes the attraction of corruptible beauty with love for Christ, who is incorruptible beauty.

The secret here is the Holy Spirit: He is the one who radiates Christ's beauty throughout the Church. He is the creator Spirit, who continually filters the world and all that it contains. He takes creation from chaos to cosmos, from ugliness to beauty, from material beauty to spiritual beauty, as at the beginning of the world. All beauty that anyone has created comes from him, just as "every truth, by whomsoever uttered, is by the Holy Spirit."[21]

Whoever "is united to the Lord becomes one spirit with him" (1 Cor 6:17). Thanks to Eucharistic communion, not only can we contemplate uncreated Beauty; we can also unite ourselves to him. The earthly union of a husband and wife is but a figure and a symbol of this union with God (see Eph 5:31-32; 1 Cor 6:16-17).

Goethe echoes this thought when he calls the earthly love of Faust for Margherita "only a symbol" ("*nur ein Gleichnis*") when compared to the final love that is transfigured in God:

> All that is transitory
> Is only a symbol;
> What seems inachieveable
> Here is seen done;
> What's indescribable
> Here becomes fact;
> Woman, eternally,
> Shows us the way.[22]

Honoring Holy Women

When speaking about the "eternal woman," our thoughts turn immediately to Mary, the *tota pulchra* or "most beautiful" as she is called in the liturgy. Devotion to the Virgin Mary is one of the most effective rationales for elevating feminine beauty instead of seeing it as an obstacle to holiness. As Luther wrote, "No image of a woman stirs up thoughts so pure in man as that virgin."[23] This devotion to Mary was responsible for creating the image of the angelic woman (such as Dante's Beatrice) in the Middle Ages, whose simple and plain appearance directed our attention to God.

It is vitally important for any young priest to attain a peaceful relationship with the feminine component of the larger Christian community, which is generally the most active group in a parish and the group that is most willing and prepared to work with a priest. Our thoughts turn to Clare, Francis' *twin soul.* The example of her relationship with Francis has something important to teach us priests.

Saint-Exupéry once wrote that "love does not consist of looking at one another, but looking together in the same direction." Clare and Francis reached this goal in a most sublime way. Furthermore, we know where they were both looking—at Jesus! They were looking at the Jesus who was poor, humble, and crucified.

Clare and Francis were like two eyes that were always looking in the same direction. Yet these two eyes were not seeing the same thing in the same way. When two eyes are fixed on an object from different angles, they make it possible for us to see that object in a different way and in a different dimension. Clare and Francis looked at the same crucifix, the same

Eucharist, creation's same beauty, and the same Lady Poverty, but from different angles and with different feelings: those of a man and those of a woman. Together they were able to understand much more than two Francises or two Clares would have been able to understand.

It is precisely this mystery of complementing each other that the Bible highlights when we read: "God created man in his own image, in the image of God he created him; male and female he created them" (Gn 1:27). A true and complete image of God does not consist of man or woman separately but the two together, each one looking at the other and each one helping the other get out of himself or herself.

A friendship between a young priest and a young woman that is exclusive and private opens the door to a dangerous alliance. Clare and Francis point the way to a redeemed beauty, not only in people but in relationships. Their unique friendship enveloped their communities. Francis became the brother and the father of all the sisters; Clare became the sister and the mother of all the friars.

Loving

Finally, there is another way of participating in the paschal mystery of redemption of beauty that is very important: accepting those who, like Christ during his passion, have "no form or comeliness that we should look at" them (Is 53:2).

These are the poor, the crucified, the people in our communities who have been abandoned. The image of Mother Teresa of Calcutta, with all her wrinkles, holding a sick child or an abandoned, dying man in her arms with infinite tenderness, is part of this beauty that has been redeemed and that is redeeming.

To respond to Dostoevski's question, therefore, it is not love of beauty that will save the world, but the beauty of love.

The Testament of St. Francis (1226)

This is how God inspired me, Brother Francis, to embark upon a life of penance. When I was in sin, the sight of lepers nauseated me beyond measure; but then God himself led me into their company, and I had pity on them. When I had once become acquainted with them, what had previously nauseated me became a source of spiritual and physical consolation for me. After that I did not wait long before leaving the world.

And God inspired me with such faith in his churches that I used to pray with all simplicity, saying, "We adore you, Lord Jesus Christ, here and in all your churches in the whole world, and we bless you, because by your holy cross you have redeemed the world."

God inspired me, too, and still inspires me with such great faith in priests who live according to the laws of the holy Church of Rome, because of their dignity, that if they persecuted me, I should still be ready to turn to them for aid. And if I were as wise as Solomon and met the poorest priests of the world, I would still refuse to preach against their will in the parishes in which they live.

I am determined to reverence, love, and honor priests and all others as my superiors. I refuse to consider their sins, because I can see the Son of God in them and they are better than I. I do this because in this world I cannot see the most high Son of God with my own eyes, except for his most holy Body and Blood, which they receive and they alone administer to others.

Above everything else, I want this most holy Sacrament to be honored and venerated and reserved in places which are richly ornamented. Whenever I find his most holy name or writings containing his words in an improper place, I make a point of picking them up, and I ask that they be picked up and put aside in a suitable place. We should honor and venerate theologians, too, and the ministers of God's word, because it is they who give us spirit and life.

When God gave me some friars, there was no one to tell me what I should do; but the Most High himself made it clear to me that I must live the life of the Gospel. I had this written down briefly and simply, and his holiness the Pope confirmed it for me. Those who embraced this life gave everything they had to the poor. They were satisfied with one habit, which was patched inside and outside, and a cord, and trousers. We refused to have anything more.

Those of us who were clerics said the Office like other clerics, while the lay brothers said the Our Father, and we were only too glad to find shelter in abandoned churches. We made no claim to learning, and we were submissive to everyone. I worked with my own hands, and I am still determined to work; and with all my heart I want all the other friars to be busy with some kind of work that can be carried on without scandal. Those who do not know how to work should learn, not because they want to get something for their efforts, but to give good example and to avoid idleness. When we receive no recompense for our work, we can turn to God's table and beg alms from door to door. God revealed a form of greeting to me, telling me that we should say, "God give you peace."

The friars must be very careful not to accept churches or poor dwellings for themselves, or anything else built for them, unless they are in harmony with the poverty which we have promised in the Rule; and they should occupy these places only as *strangers and pilgrims* [see 1 Pt 2:11].

In virtue of obedience, I strictly forbid the friars, wherever they may be, to petition the Roman Curia, either personally or through an intermediary, for a papal brief, whether it concerns a church or any other place, or even in order to preach, or because they are being persecuted. If they are not welcome somewhere, they should flee to another country where they can lead a life of penance, with God's blessing.

I am determined to obey the Minister General of the Order and the guardians whom he sees fit to give me. I want to be a captive in his hands so that I cannot travel about or do anything against his command or desire, because he is my superior. Although I am ill and not much use, I always want to have a cleric with me who will say the office for me, as is prescribed in the Rule.

All the other friars, too, are bound to obey their guardians in the same way, and say the Office according to the Rule. If any of them refuse to say the Office according to the Rule and want to change it, or if they are not true to the Catholic faith, the other friars are bound in virtue of obedience to bring them before the *custos* nearest the place where they find them. The *custos* must keep any such friar as a prisoner day and night so that he cannot escape from his hands until he personally hands him over to his minister. The minister, then, is strictly bound by obedience to place him in the care of the friars, who will guard him day and night like a prisoner until they present him before his lordship the Bishop of Ostia, who is the superior, protector, and corrector of the whole Order.

The friars should not say this is another Rule. For this is a reminder, admonition, exhortation, and my testament which I, brother Francis, worthless as I am, leave to you, my brothers, that we may observe in a more Catholic way the Rule we have promised to God. The Minister General and all the other ministers and custodies are bound in virtue of obedience not to add anything to these words or subtract from them. They should always have this writing with them as well as the Rule, and at the chapters they hold, when the Rule is read, they should read these words also.

In virtue of obedience, I strictly forbid any of my friars, clerics, or lay brothers to interpret the Rule or these words, saying, "This is what they mean." God inspired me to write the Rule and these words plainly and simply, and so you too must understand them plainly and simply, and live by them, doing good to the last.

And may whoever observes all this be filled in heaven with the blessing of the most high Father, and on earth with that of his beloved Son, together with the Holy Spirit, the Comforter, and all the powers of heaven and all the saints. And I, Brother Francis, your poor worthless servant, add my share internally and externally to that most holy blessing. Amen.[24]

"This Is My Testament"
Francis Speaks to Priests Today

Raniero Cantalamessa

This is the second meditation given at the Monastery of La Verna on the morning of February 16, 2000.

I believe that the fundamental reason why you chose La Verna for your annual pilgrimage was so that you could listen to Francis. The reason I agreed to come here was so that I could let him speak to you as directly as possible.

At one point I had considered speaking about Francis and the renewal of the Church, based on the words that Jesus spoke to him from the Cross of San Damiano: "Go, Francis, and rebuild my Church." I even wrote a few pages for such a talk, but then I tore them up. I realized that the talk was turning out to be a sort of tribute to St. Francis, something that smacks of religious parochialism and does not seem very credible when coming from the mouth of a Franciscan. More than anything, though, such a talk would leave less room for Francis to speak about himself and about problems concerning the Church today.

This is a unique opportunity to let the *Poverello* himself speak to you young priests. Like many other pilgrims, we are here as Elisha. We hope to pick up the mantel of Elijah, a little part of his spirit. (One tradition in iconography identifies Francis as the new Elijah. Giotto portrayed this in a fresco depicting St. Francis dressed as the new Elijah, ascending into heaven in a chariot of fire.)

The surest way to let Francis speak to us is to spend some time reading his *Testament*. Since it was written a few weeks before he died, many people feel that it faithfully mirrors his soul. They feel that this document is the one that is freest from any outside influence and that most reflects both his personality and his message. St. Francis himself tells us that it is "a reminder, admonition, exhortation, and my testament which I, Brother Francis, worthless as I am, leave to you, my brothers, that we may observe in a more Catholic way the Rule we have promised to God."[1]

We Franciscans read the *Testament* right after reading the Rule, as Francis himself said we should. However, as we shall see, this is not only a *Testament* for his friars; it is a word that Francis had for the entire Church. It is in this spirit that we wish to meditate upon it now.

We will recall Francis' great loves as reflected in this document. We will not meditate upon them in his absence but in his presence. He is with us thanks to the mystery of the communion of saints, and thanks, too, to the love that he has for this "rough rock 'twixt Tiber and Arno shore" where "he took the final imprint of the rood from Christ."[2]

A Love for Lepers

Francis' *Testament* begins on an autobiographical note:

> This is how God inspired me, Brother Francis, to embark upon a life of penance. When I was in sin, the sight of lepers nauseated me beyond measure; but then God himself led me into their company, and I had pity on them. When I had once become acquainted with them, what had previously nauseated me became a source of spiritual and physical consolation for me. After that I did not wait long before leaving the world.[3]

This is the account of his conversion. These few lines capture the long process in which grace was slowly and intensely at work to snatch him from his carefree and worldly life (but not a dissolute life, as many people who like to exaggerate have said at times). Francis was on the path to a future full of fame and feasting when he began to feel a strange void.

Many experience this void, but few know how to find the

right outlet for it. They tend to fill it with other things. But for Francis, dreams that once had the power to catalyze all his thoughts began to fade away: chivalry, love, and military adventure. It was the dark night of the senses, when the promises and pleasures of the world begin to lose their appeal for the soul.

This is the situation in which he found himself when the Lord began to visit him. God gently and quietly began to send him some signs. God does not wish to force people to choose; he wants to win them over. He wins them through attraction rather than constraint.

So while Francis was at Foligno, he had a dream. In that dream he saw some incredible weapons, and he heard the Lord ask him if it would be better to serve "the servant or the lord." The "servant" was Gualtieri di Brienne. Francis was a member of his entourage at that time.[4]

It was at this time, too, that Francis was captured in battle and imprisoned at Perugia. There he had time to reflect on his life. God's grace and man's freedom were progressively drawing closer to each other, leading up to that crucial moment when God's creature would determine his fate for eternity.

The Encounter

That moment came when Francis met the leper. If there was anything that Francis dreaded (as he himself said), it was the sight of lepers, even from a distance. He was about to run away from the leper when a force began to work within him. This force, alien to his nature, led him to stop, turn around, and get off his horse. Then he offered the leper alms and kissed him.

Francis described this episode in his life in rather terse words: "I had pity on them." However, various Franciscan writers tell us the full story. Francis did not simply kiss the leper and forget about him or about this meeting with him. This episode was the beginning of a relationship between him and lepers that continued throughout his entire life. He called lepers "my Christian brothers." As Tommaso da Celano writes:

> Then the holy lover of complete humility went to the lepers and lived with them, serving them most diligently for God's sake; and washing all foulness from them, he wiped away also the corruption of the ulcers. So greatly loathsome was the sight of lepers to him at one time, he used to say, that, in the days of his vanity, he would look at their houses only from a distance of two miles and he would hold his nostrils with his hands. But now, when by the grace and power of the Most High he was beginning to think of holy and useful things, while he was still clad in secular garments, he met a leper one day and, made stronger than himself, he kissed him. From then on he began to despise himself more and more, until, by the mercy of the Redeemer, he came to perfect victory over himself.[5]

It would be easy to misinterpret Francis' gesture by simply reducing it to an expression of his sensitivity for the poor and the afflicted. It has been said at times that Francis' conversion to the poor was the determining factor in his conversion to God. But the importance of this moment lies elsewhere.

Francis, in kissing the leper, overcame his own desires. He made a choice between himself and God—between saving his life or losing it. He was "made stronger than himself," as Tommaso da Celano noted, thereby laying the foundation for following Christ by denying himself (see Mk 8:34).

His great venture into holiness began with a victory over his own self. This is true conversion.

This does not mean that our neighbor (in this case the leper) is not important in his own right. On the contrary. Saying no to oneself and saying yes to one's neighbor are two sides of the same coin, two aspects of the same decision. The first is the means, and the second is the end.

In Christianity, self-denial is not an end in itself. Rather, it is the most perfect way of opening ourselves up to others and to God. In order to help others, we first of all need to die to ourselves. This is the way in which we incarnate the fundamental law of Christian sacrifice, in which the *recipient* of the sacrifice is God but the *beneficiary* is one's neighbor. This parallels Christ's handing himself over to the Father for us (see Eph 5:2).

A Model for Us

Let's consider how Francis' first love can be incorporated into the life of a priest. Ever since biblical times, the leper has been a symbol of rejection, suffering, and extreme poverty. Thus it is easy to translate this story into a more modern context characterized by other forms of rejection, suffering, and poverty.

Francis reminds us that love for the poor—today's lepers—should be among a priest's loves. But this love should be the fruit of conversion to the gospel and not merely a choice made on the basis of some argument or principle of sociology.

Francis saw his approach of the leper as the moment when he "left the world." His decision was not inspired by some mundane reason, be it compassion or pity.

Furthermore, our celebrations of the Eucharist should spur us priests on to help the poor and the suffering. At every Mass we repeat the words: "Take this and eat of it, this is my body." We who utter these words over the bread have also uttered them over the *lepers*—the hungry, the naked, the sick, the imprisoned. For Christ has said, whatever we have done or not done for these, we have done or not done for him (see Mt 25:31-46). This is tantamount to saying, "That naked body, that famished body, that wounded body that you found, was my body. It was I."

Therefore, love for the poor and the suffering is an integral part of our priestly ministry, even though the ways of putting it into practice have changed. We cannot do everything ourselves. Yet there is at least one thing that depends largely on priests. We need to make sure that the poor and the forsaken feel comfortable in our gatherings, that they do not feel any discrimination in our churches. St. James' admonition to us is timely:

> For if a man with gold rings and in fine clothing comes into your assembly, and a poor man in shabby clothing also comes in, and you pay attention to the one who wears the fine clothing and say, "Have a seat here, please," while you say to the poor man, "Stand there," or, "Sit at my feet," have you not made distinctions among yourselves, and become judges with evil thoughts?
>
> JAMES 2:2-4

A Love for Priests

Let us look at Francis' second love in his *Testament:*

> God inspired me, too, and still inspires me with such great faith in priests who live according to the laws of the holy Church of Rome, because of their dignity, that if they persecuted me, I should still be ready to turn to them for aid. And if I were as wise as Solomon and met the poorest priests of the world, I would still refuse to

preach against their will in the parishes in which they live. I am determined to reverence, love and honor priests and all others as my superiors. I refuse to consider their sins, because I can see the Son of God in them and they are better than I.[6]

Francis' love for priests was even more surprising when you consider the era in which he was writing. B. Cornet has described the condition of the clergy during Francis' time, based on canons from the councils and decrees from the popes.[7] There was an enormous difference between the higher clergy, which moved among the privileged, and the ordinary clergy, which was left to its own resources.

The moral and intellectual situation of the lower clergy was truly deplorable. Churches were often converted into barns, and concubinage among the clergy was widespread. Criticism of the clergy was commonplace in the popular literature of the time, and on occasion people actually rebelled against their priests and forced them to flee.

Francis responded with the love that he described in his *Testament*. The *Poverello* structured his religious order on the principle that his friars should not be competing with parish priests but serving them. Thus he did not want them to have their own churches. He wanted them to have only small oratories for their personal use while they served in the existing parishes.

Francis' thoughts on loving priests are found not only in his *Testament*. The following text reveals how Francis instilled this love for priests of the diocese in his brothers:

One day, certain brothers said to blessed Francis: "Father, do you not see that the bishops sometimes refuse us permission to preach and thereby oblige us to remain several days doing nothing in a region before we can speak to the people? It would be desirable to obtain a privilege from the lord pope for the friars for the salvation of souls."

He answered them vehemently: "You, Friars Minor, do not know the will of God, and you do not let me convert the whole world as God wishes. You must first convert the prelates by your humility and your respectful obedience. When they see the holy life that you lead and the respect that you show them, they themselves will ask you to preach and convert the people; they will bring you your audience better than the privileges for which you clamor and which will lead you into pride. If you are despoiled of all cupidity, if you lead their people to respect the rights of their churches, the bishops will ask you to hear the confessions of their people.

"Furthermore, this concern should not be yours, because if sinners are converted, they will find many confessors. For myself, the privilege I ask of the Lord is never to be indebted to any man but to be subject to all and to convert the entire world in conformity with the holy rule more by example than by word."8

Francis' love for priests even extends to us, who have come to this place in order to rekindle the fire of his spirit. I hope this spirit characterizes my presence among you today.

A Love for the Eucharist

Let us look now at Francis' third love, which is closely related to the preceding love, love for the Eucharist. He used this love to justify his love for priests. In fact, he wrote:

> I do this because in this world I cannot see the most high Son of God with my own eyes, except for his most holy Body and Blood which they receive and they alone minister to others. Above everything else, I want this most holy Sacrament to be honored and venerated and reserved in places which are richly ornamented.9

In order to understand Francis' insistence on proper decorum and the respect we should show for the Blessed Sacrament, here too, we need to understand the situation at that time.

B. Cornet's study, which I referred to above, also documents the deplorable state in which people held the Eucharist, as well as the efforts of the popes and the councils to correct the more serious abuses.[10] St. Francis himself wrote about some of these abuses in a letter to the clergy:

We clerics cannot overlook the sinful neglect and ignorance some people are guilty of with regard to the holy Body and Blood of our Lord Jesus Christ....

Those who are in charge of these sacred mysteries, and especially those who are careless about their task, should realize that the chalices, corporals, and altar linens where the Body and Blood of our Lord Jesus Christ are offered in sacrifice should be completely suitable. And besides, many clerics reserve the Blessed Sacrament in unsuitable places, or carry It about irreverently, or receive It unworthily, or give It to all comers without distinction. God's holy name, too, and his written words are sometimes trodden underfoot, because *the sensual man does not perceive the things that are of the Spirit of God* (1 Cor 2:14).

Surely we cannot be left unmoved by loving sorrow for all this; in his love God gives himself into our hands; we touch him and receive him daily into our mouths. Have we forgotten that we must fall into his hands?

And so we must correct these and all other abuses. If

the Body of our Lord Jesus Christ has been left abandoned somewhere contrary to all the laws, It should be removed and put in a place that is prepared properly for It, where It can be kept safe.[11]

In this regard, as well as in many others things, Francis tried to bring about gently and carefully the liturgical reforms sanctioned by the Fourth Lateran Council, especially concerning Canons 19 and 20.[12]

Honor the Eucharist

Francis' insistence on exterior decorum, even if rooted in some of the particular problems of his times, is still important for us priests today. People instinctively measure the faith of a priest according to the way he conducts himself in the presence of the Blessed Sacrament and the care that he gives to the altar and the tabernacle (a flower, if only one, but always fresh!). One genuflection can say more to people than an entire sermon on the real presence.

But Francis' love and zeal for the Eucharist has some even deeper motives. For the Eucharist is Christ present in his "most holy Body." St. Leo the Great said that "everything that was visible to you of our Lord Jesus Christ after his Ascension was incorporated into sacramental signs."[13]

Francis' tender love for the Child Jesus and for Jesus crucified—

"the humility of the incarnation and the charity of the passion"[14]—were all contained in the Eucharist. For Francis, the Eucharist is not simply a ritual, a mystery, a truth, a dogma, or a sacrament, even if it is the most sublime of all. The Eucharist is a humble, defenseless, living person. It is, as one of the Eucharistic prayers says, God who places his body in our hands.

Let us consider some of Francis' own words on how to rekindle this fire in our lives:

Listen to this, my brothers: If it is right to honor the Blessed Virgin Mary because she bore him in her most holy womb; if St. John the Baptist trembled and was afraid even to touch Christ's sacred head (see Mt 3:13-14); if the tomb where he lay for only a short time is so venerated; how holy, and virtuous, and worthy should not a priest be; he touches Christ with his own hands, Christ who is to die now no more but enjoy eternal life and glory, *upon whom the angels desire to look* (1 Pt 1:12). A priest receives him into his heart and mouth and offers him to others to be received.

Remember your dignity, then, my friar-priests. *You shall make and keep yourselves holy,* because God is holy (Lv 11:44). In this mystery God has honored you above all other human beings, and so you must love, revere, and honor him more than all others. Surely this is a great pity, a pitiable weakness, to have him present with you like this and be distracted by anything else in the whole world. Our whole being should be seized with fear, the whole world should tremble and heaven rejoice, when Christ the Son of the living God is present on the altar in the hands of the priest.

What wonderful majesty! What stupendous condescension! O sublime humility! O humble sublimity! That the Lord of the whole universe, God and the Son of God, should humble himself like this and hide under the form of a little bread, for our salvation. Look at God's condescension, my brothers, and *pour out your hearts before him* (Ps 62:8). Humble yourselves that you may be exalted by him (see 1 Pt 5:6). Keep nothing for yourselves, so that he who has given himself wholly to you may receive you wholly.[15]

Be Eucharist

The link between the Eucharist and the life of a priest is expressed in this last sentence. A priest cannot simply be satisfied with celebrating the Eucharist; he must *be* Eucharist. The words that the bishop said over us at the time of our ordination were *"Agnoscite quod agitis, imitamini quod tractatis,"* which means, "Recognize what you are doing, imitate (in your life) what you are doing (on the altar)."

A great spiritual teacher, Fr. Olivaint, once said: "In the morning, I'm the priest and he (Jesus) is the victim; during the day, he (Jesus) is the priest and I'm the victim *(Le matin, moi prêtre, lui victime; le long du jour lui prêtre, moi victime)*."

Many things have changed in me since the day I began saying the words of the consecration not only *in persona Christi*, in Christ's name, but also in my own name: "Take and eat, my brothers and sisters. This is my body—my time, my energy, my resources, and my abilities—offered as a sacrifice for you.... Take and drink, this is my blood—my sufferings, my failures, and my illnesses—poured out for you." When we take these words seriously, they can transform our entire day.

I recall the words of one parish priest, Fr. Mario from Mombello, who died a few years ago. He was suffering from a tumor that was in its final stages, and he also had an eye disease. I saw him a few days before his death. He truly seemed like Christ on the cross to me, and his words confirmed that:

Father, during a retreat for priests in the deanery, you suggested that we also say the words of the consecration in our own name, uniting ourselves to Christ: "Take and eat: this is my body.... Take and drink of my blood." I have to admit that I did not understand what you were saying at the time and I didn't attach much importance to it. But now I understand. It's the only thing that I can still do. As I'm

doing it, I am constantly thinking about my parishioners.
At that moment I saw the sublime grandeur of the life of one priest who had become a living Eucharist.

When Jesus said, "Do this in memory of me," perhaps he did not simply mean, "Do exactly what you saw me do." Perhaps he meant something more essential: "Do the essence of what I have done. I offered myself to the Father for you. You, too, must offer yourselves with me to the Father for your brothers."

This is how Paul understood Christ's words. He said, "I appeal to you therefore, brethren, by the mercies of God, to present your bodies as a living sacrifice, holy and acceptable to God, which is your spiritual worship" (Rom 12:1).

People have said, "The Eucharist makes the Church." This is true. But now we know how the Eucharist makes the Church. The Eucharist makes the Church by making the Church a Eucharist!

A Love for God's Word

Francis' love for the Eucharist was inseparable from his love for God's word. Recall these words from his *Testament:*

Whenever I find his most holy name or writings containing his words in an improper place, I make a point of picking them up, and I ask that they be picked up and put aside in a suitable place. We should honor and venerate theologians, too, and the ministers of God's word, because it is they who give us spirit and life.[16]

Francis speaks about the "fragrant words of my Lord" in one of his letters,[17] implicitly comparing God's word to fragrant loaves of bread. Another letter to his friars includes a vibrant passage on God's Word:

I urge all my friars and I encourage them in Christ to show all possible respect for God's words wherever they may happen to find them in writing. If they are not kept properly or if they lie thrown about disrespectfully, they should pick them up and put them aside, paying honor in his words to God who spoke them. God's words sanctify numerous objects (1 Tm 4:5), and it is by the power of the words of Christ that the sacrament of the altar is consecrated.[18]

According to Francis, God's Word, just like God's mysteries, is an aspect of Christ's living presence. This is why he wants us to find concrete ways in which we can materially care for God's Word. For Francis, God's Word is a reality that he can almost feel, just as we can feel God's Word in the Bible, where it "falls upon"

Israel, "comes to" or "settles upon" the prophet, and is active and operative like the rain, a fire, or a hammer (see Jer 23:29).

Francis experienced the power of the Word in his life, and he recalls this in his *Testament:*

> When God gave me some friars, there was no one to tell me what I should do; but the Most High himself made it clear to me that I must live the life of the Gospel. I had this written down briefly and simply, and his holiness the Pope confirmed it for me.[19]

This passage alludes to a well-known story in which Francis randomly opened the Gospels and received a threefold confirmation of what he should do.[20] We might have some reservations about this method of using Scripture, but the history of the Church is full of such stories, which often mark the beginning of a new vocation or a new life. This is how St. Anthony's vocation as a hermit originated. This is what brought about St. Augustine's conversion. St. Thérèse of Lisieux discovered her vocation in the Church as she read 1 Corinthians 12–13.

I was personally involved in such an incident. I had preached a mission in Australia for a group of Italians there. The evening before the last day, a man came to me—a simple worker—and said: "Father, I have a problem in my family. I have an eleven-year-old son who is not baptized. However, my wife became a Jehovah's Witness and doesn't want him baptized. If I have him baptized, I'm afraid that this will upset our family life. If I don't have him baptized, I won't feel peaceful because we were both Catholic when we married and we both made a commitment to have our children baptized."

I told the man to let me think about it. The next day he came up to me beaming and said, "Father, I found the answer. Last night I opened the Bible to the story of Abraham and read how Abraham was going to sacrifice his son, Isaac, without telling his wife."

I was dumbfounded. From an exegetical point of view, this reading was perfect. I personally baptized the boy, and we had a big celebration.

There are numerous cases in which simple people have opened the Bible in faith and, after praying, have found clear indications of God's will for their lives. It is not necessary or advisable to always resort to this method. There are times when we should randomly *listen* to Scripture instead of randomly *opening* it. We need to listen to Scripture with open ears so that we might recognize God's Word for us as it is being proclaimed, for example in the liturgy.

In fact, according to Celano, the threefold random confirmation of the Gospels was not the determining factor in Francis' decision in life. Rather, Celano highlighted the fact that Francis made his choice in life during Mass, when he heard the Gospel account of Christ's invitation to the apostles.[21] "For he was not a deaf hearer of the Gospel," his biographer concluded, "but committing all that he had heard to praiseworthy memory, he tried diligently to carry it out to the letter."[22] We have to listen attentively in order to respond *at once* to God's Word to us amid everything else we hear or read.

I cannot end this reflection on Francis' love for God's Word without directing an urgent plea to my fellow priests. Administer "God's most holy words" to the people; be preachers of the Word. Defend the prophetic anointing that you received during your ordination to the priesthood. It is easy to let yourself be completely absorbed by other tasks—"to serve tables"—and neglect "prayer and the ministry of the word" (Acts 6:2, 4).

The Word is the principal means of attracting people to the gospel and bringing them to God. "So faith comes from what is heard, and what is heard comes by the preaching of Christ" (Rom 10:17). The Word is the plow that tills the earth and cuts furrows. Everything else follows: liturgy, catechesis, exhortations, works of charity—everything.

Proclaiming the Word is where priests can experience fatherhood most clearly. As Paul told the Corinthians, "I became your father in Christ Jesus through the gospel" (1 Cor 4:15). Many priests experience a crisis because they do not have the thrilling experience of this type of fatherhood, which is so different from fleshly fatherhood yet is just as real and infinitely deeper. "You have been born anew, not of perishable seed but of imperishable, through the living and abiding word of God" (1 Pt 1:23).

You have heard what Francis said about theologians and why he felt they should be honored and respected. All priests are theologians, for a theologian is a person who proclaims God's Word and gives "spirit and life" to his people.

A Love for "Lady Poverty"

Finally, let us read what Francis had to say in his *Testament* about his love for Lady Poverty:

The friars must be very careful not to accept churches or poor dwellings for themselves, or anything else built for them, unless they are in harmony with the poverty which we have promised in the Rule; and they should occupy these places only as *strangers and pilgrims* [see 1 Pt 2:11].

In virtue of obedience, I strictly forbid the friars, wherever they may be, to petition the Roman Curia, either personally or through an intermediary, for a papal brief, whether it concerns a church or any other place, or even in order to preach, or because they are being persecuted. If they are not welcome somewhere, they should flee to another country where they can lead a life of penance, with God's blessing.[23]

St. Bonaventure summed up Francis' love for poverty in a well-known chapter in his *Major Life of St. Francis*. He highlighted its most inner, spiritual aspect: the poverty of prestige and love for one's self. Anyone who wishes to form a less superficial and less stereotyped idea of Francis' poverty should read this chapter.[24] We will glance at a few passages in our effort to draw nearer to the Poverello. We can only do so by taking an interest in what Dante calls "his most dear lady," which Francis entrusted to his brothers as his rightful heirs ("*giusta rede*").[25]

No one was so greedy for gold as Francis was for poverty; no one treasure was guarded as jealously as he guarded this gospel pearl. He used to be particularly offended if ever he saw anything contrary to poverty among the friars. From the first moment of his religious life until his death, his sole wealth consisted in a habit, a cord, and a pair of trousers, and he was content with that.

The memory of the poverty felt by Christ and his Mother often reduced him to tears, and he called poverty the Queen of the Virtues because it was so evident in the life of the King of Kings and of the Queen, his Mother....

It was in poverty that he chose to surpass others, because it had shown him how to regard himself as the last of all. Whenever he saw anyone who was more poorly dressed than he, he immediately reproached himself and roused himself to imitate him. He was jealous of his poverty and he was afraid of being outdone, as he fought to deserve it. One day he met a beggar on the road and when he saw how poorly dressed he was, his heart was touched and he exclaimed sorrowfully to his companion, "His poverty puts us to shame. We have chosen poverty as our wealth, and look, it is more resplendent in him."[26]

Francis entrusted his love for poverty not only to "his friars" but to all of Christ's followers, especially his priests.

Poverty of Power

Perhaps the most profound and most original aspect of Francis' poverty was poverty of power and dominion. This was why, in his *Testament*, he forbade his friars to have recourse to any of their ecclesiastical privileges. Clearly he saw this as a dark evil that accounted for so many enemies and so much opposition to the Church in his day.

Jesus substituted service for dominion (see Mk 10:42-45).

Little by little, though, people had returned to a worldly concept of authority. Francis was unrelenting on this point. He called his friars "servants of all people" and referred to himself as "your servant." In his order, religious superiors were not called abbots, priors, or prelates but *ministers*, which means "servants." The superiors were "ministers and servants of the other friars."27

This aspect of poverty is important for priests. They are also called to *ministry*, to *service*. Like so many other words, the world has changed the meaning of *ministry*. We talk about the Ministry of Finance, the Ministry of the Treasury, the Ministry of Internal Affairs, and the Ministry of Foreign Affairs. All these expressions do not quite convey the idea of humble service.

St. Paul clearly perceived this as a threat to the apostles' ministry: "Not that we lord it over your faith; we work with you for your joy" (2 Cor 1:24). Along the same lines, Peter exhorted the presbyters not to lord it over those assigned to them but to be examples to the flock (see 1 Pt 5:2-3).

Why is it that many people in some of the most traditionally "Catholic" countries have turned their backs on the Church in such a dramatic way? I once posed this question to a priest in Holland. His response was thought-provoking. He told me that the priest had been everything for people in Holland: He made every decision, even in the areas of marriage and family life. As people's dependence on the priest dissipated over time and as the culture evolved, people moved to the opposite extreme. They rejected everything.

I believe that this explains at least in part the crisis that one country after another has encountered over time—countries such as Ireland, Holland, and Spain that were once strongholds of Catholicism. People's indifference to the Church began with an indifference among the clergy.

Think about how the premises and, more particularly, the resources of our parishes are generally handled. People need to understand that the pastor of the parish is not the owner of the parish. The parish's resources are not his things that he lends to others out of the goodness of his heart. Rather, priests are simply keepers of the Lord's courts (see Zec 3:7). Of course, as such they need to see to it that the Church's property and resources are used correctly insofar as possible. But they also need to let the people know that this property belongs to everyone.

The Lord Is Our Inheritance

There is a positive way in which a priest can understand Francis' love of poverty. It is in having God as the only portion of his inheritance. Poverty is within his grasp, more so than its opposite. Through poverty he can give up everything in order to have everything!

When the Promised Land was divided, we know that no portion of the land was assigned to the priests or to the Levites because the Lord was to be their inheritance. The portions of land were assigned by drawing lots. For this reason the Levites said that their good fortune was to have the place of their delight. God was the place of their delight.

What God told Aaron back then, Christ is telling priests in his Church today: "I am your portion and your inheritance among the people of Israel" (Nm 18:20). It is good to recall, in this respect, that the words *clergyman* and *cleric* are derived from the word *inheritance*, which is *kleros* in Greek.

Francis' *Testament* ends with a long blessing, which he surely extends to all who have heard his words and who share his "loves":

And may whoever observes all this be filled in heaven with the blessing of the most high Father, and on earth with that of his beloved Son, together with the Holy Spirit, the Comforter, and all the powers of heaven and all the saints. And I, Brother Francis, your poor worthless servant, add my share internally and externally to that most holy blessing. Amen.[28]

The Miracle of the Stigmata and the Manner in Which the Seraph Appeared to Him

Tommaso da Celano

This is how the apparition occurred. Two years before rendering his spirit up to heaven, on a high mountain called La Verna in Tuscany where he could be alone in devout contemplation, he was directing all his attention to the celestial glory when he saw above him in a vision a Seraph with six wings, with his hands and feet stretched out and nailed to a cross. Two of the wings were raised above his head and two were stretched out in flight, while the remaining two shielded his body.

Francis was dumbfounded at the sight, and his heart was flooded with a mixture of joy and sorrow. He was overjoyed at the way Christ regarded him so graciously under the appearance of a Seraph, but the fact that he was nailed to a cross pierced his soul with a sword of compassionate sorrow. Immediately he sought to understand the significance of this vision, and his soul anxiously tried to find some explanation. Looking for an explanation outside himself, his intellect was of little use. Immediately the meaning appeared on his very own body.

Then and there the marks of the nails began to

appear in his hands and feet, just as he had seen them in his vision of the man nailed to the cross. His hands and feet appeared pierced through the center with nails, the heads of which were in the palms of his hands and on the instep of each foot, while the points stuck out on the opposite side. The heads were black and round, but the points were long and bent back; they rose above the surrounding flesh and stood out from it. His right side seemed as if it had been pierced with a lance and was marked with a livid scar which often bled, so that his habit and trousers were stained.

In fact, Rufino, that man of God who was of an angelic purity, was taking care of our holy father with filial love when his hand slipped and touched this very sensitive wound. This servant of God suffered greatly because of this, and, moving his hand away, moaned and prayed that the Lord would forgive him for this.

Two years later [Francis] peacefully passed from the valley of tears to his blessed homeland. When the wonderful news reached the ears of the townspeople, all the people came to see, praising and glorifying God's name. All the citizens of Assisi and the surrounding regions came, wishing to see the new miracle that God had performed in this world.

The miracle was so extraordinary that their tears were

transformed into joy as they beheld his body in amazement and ecstasy. Thus, they contemplated his blessed
body made precious by the wounds of Christ. They did
not merely see the holes in his hands and feet from the
nails, but the nails themselves formed out of his flesh by
God; they were so much part of his flesh that, when they
were pressed on one side, they immediately jutted out
further on the other side. They also saw the red wound
in his side.

We saw these things with our own eyes. The hands
with which we are writing touched the wounds, and the
testimony that we give with our lips we saw with tears in
our eyes. We confirmed all this for eternity with an oath
we made by touching sacred objects. Many friars besides
me, while the Saint was alive, saw the same thing; when
he died, another fifty friars and numerous lay people
venerated his body.

There is no uncertainty or doubt of God's eternal
goodness! It is God's will that many members of Christ's
body adhere to their head, who is Christ, with the same
seraphic love, so that they are found worthy to wear the
same armor in the battle and will be raised to the same
glory in the Kingdom! How could any in his right mind
not claim that this was anything but the glory of Christ?[29]

Man's Wisdom and Power, God's Weakness and Foolishness

Obedience and Resistance to the Word of the Cross

Carlo Maria Martini

Cardinal Carlo Maria Martini retired in July 2002, after twenty years of service as the archbishop of Milan. He has been active in the Curia and has authored several books. He gave this meditation at the Monastery of La Verna the afternoon of February 16, 2000.

I am very happy to return to this place, where I had a very moving experience many years ago. I had the same experience once again when I read two books.

The first was a two-act play by Alighiero Chiusano called *Le notti della Verna (Nights at La Verna)*. In this play Francis' visits to La Verna, especially his last visit, are compared to the vigil that Jesus kept in the Garden of Gethsemane.

The other book was E. Leclerc's *La sapienza di un povero (Wisdom of a Poor Man)*. Here the author attempts to relive the nights that Francis spent at La Verna contemplating the mystery of his stigmata.

We have gathered here in order to learn how to pray before our crucified Lord—to pray before the cross, through the mystery of the stigmata. Fr. Cantalamessa has already introduced you to the meaning of Francis' presence. I have been entrusted with the difficult theme of "Man's Wisdom and Power, God's Weakness and Foolishness: Obedience and Resistance to the Word of the Cross."

This topic is truly overwhelming. To avoid the risk of sounding superficial or rhetorical, I have asked St. Francis, St. Charles Borromeo, St. Teresa Benedicta of the Cross, and some other saints who had the gift of contemplating the wisdom of the cross to intercede for me.

Personally I feel very attracted to the mystery of the cross. I feel it is the key to salvation history, and I have addressed this topic on many occasions. For example, the following passage from the *Rule of Life for an Ambrosian Christian* was included in a section called "The 'Suffering' God and the Law of the Cross":

I would like ... everyone to understand that the mystery of a God who has died and risen from the dead is the key to human existence, as well as the essence of the gospel and our faith! Nonetheless, we resist with all our strength this rock of the "Paschal Mystery...."

Yet this is the place where all the bonds of relationship join together, linking life and death, joy and suffering, failure and success, frustration and desire, humiliation and exaltation, hope and desperation. The "Law of the Cross" is unsettling. It deeply disturbs us. But it is through the cross that we are completely delivered from sin, insofar as we accept its effectiveness for forgiving sin and overcome sin just as Jesus did on the cross.[1]

I would like to do a very simple meditation with you. After an introduction to Philippians 3:18 (on the enemies of the cross), we will devote some time to a *lectio* (reading) and a *meditatio* (meditation) on 1 Corinthians 1–2.

Introduction: The Enemies of the Cross

"Many, of whom I have often told you and now tell you even with tears, live as enemies of the cross of Christ" (Phil 3:18).

This verse from Scripture is thought-provoking. St. Paul, speaking about the Christian community, states rather categorically that many people do not understand the mystery of the cross. Furthermore, the verb that is translated here as "live" literally means "are walking." It refers to an enmity to the cross that is manifested in the daily lifestyle of many people who call themselves Christians.

We should also note that Paul had denounced this error

"often." It weighed heavily on his heart. Now he repeats his warning "with tears." He is weeping tears of sorrow, just as he wept tears of sorrow as he reflected on Israel's fate in Romans 9.

Who are the enemies of the cross of Christ? Instinctively we think of those people who lead sinful and licentious lives—people who have a hedonistic vision of life. In reality, though, this passage refers to a few people who have formed rival factions, and Paul weeps when he sees them making sacrifices that are useless and harmful.

Concretely, the enemies are the Judaizers whom we read about at the beginning of Philippians 3: "Look out for the dogs, look out for the evil-workers, look out for those who mutilate the flesh" (verse 2). These people are convinced that they can be saved through their own works and sacrifices, through circumcision and observance of the law. They do not have faith in the cross of Jesus.

The fact that this is the kind of Christian that Paul had in mind is confirmed in verse 19, where he describes them by their three characteristics: "Their end is destruction, their god is the belly [they expect to be saved by observing dietary laws on what is pure and what is impure], and they glory in their shame [the sign of circumcision on their bodies], with minds set on earthly things [they are tied down to human observances]." Immediately afterward he adds: "But our commonwealth is in heaven" (verse 20).

It is not easy to recognize the enemies of the cross of Christ based on any preconceived notions. One exegete describes them in these terms: "They refuse the cross as the key to interpreting Christian life, and they are entirely taken up by the idea of being able to take an enthusiastic part in the triumphant and victorious glory of the Resurrected Christ at the present time."

Using language that is more familiar to us, we can pick out three different categories of people who are enemies of the cross.

1. The first group, which St. Paul zeroes in on in this text, consists of people who seek to justify themselves through the works of the law and who refuse the salvation that comes from God's unique, forgiving love.

2. There are also those who are completely closed to the idea of a crucified God. They refute the fact that the cross is God's chosen way to redeem the world and the way for interpreting life according to God's plan.

3. Then there are those who refute the mystery of the cross itself. They do not wish to take up the cross and associate themselves with Jesus' love. This is contrary to Paul's experience: "Now I rejoice in my sufferings for

your sake, and in my flesh I complete what is lacking in Christ's afflictions for the sake of his body, that is, the Church" (Col 1:24).

This third category is rather broad and should be clarified theologically. It does not refer in some simplistic way to people who lack a spirit of sacrifice. It refers, above all, to those who lack faith in God—a God who loves us dearly and forgives us.

Before examining this passage in greater detail, it is profitable to conduct a *lectio divina* on another passage, 1 Corinthians 1:17–2:5.

The Text

For Christ did not send me to baptize but to preach the gospel, and not with eloquent wisdom, lest the cross of Christ be emptied of its power.

For the word of the cross is folly to those who are perishing, but to us who are being saved it is the power of God. For it is written, "I will destroy the wisdom of the wise, and the cleverness of the clever I will thwart." Where is the wise man? Where is the scribe? Where is the debater of this age? Has not God made foolish the wisdom of the world? For since, in the wisdom of God, the world did not know God through wisdom, it pleased God through the folly of what we preach to save those who believe. For Jews demand signs and Greeks seek wisdom, but we preach Christ crucified, a stumbling block to Jews and folly to Gentiles, but to those who are called, both Jews and Greeks, Christ the power of God and the wisdom of God. For the foolishness of God is wiser than men, and the weakness of God is stronger than men.

For consider your call, brethren; not many of you were wise according to worldly standards, not many were powerful, not many were of noble birth; but God chose what is foolish in the world to shame the wise, God chose what is weak in the world to shame the strong, God chose what is low and despised in the world, even things that are not, to bring to nothing things that are, so that no human being might boast in the presence of God. He is the source of your life in Christ Jesus, whom God made our wisdom, our righteousness and sanctification and redemption; therefore, as it is written, "Let him who boasts, boast of the Lord."

When I came to you, brethren, I did not come proclaiming to you the testimony of God in lofty words or wisdom. For I decided to know nothing among you except Jesus Christ and him crucified. And I was with you in weakness and in much fear and trembling; and my speech and my message were not in plausible words of wisdom, but in demonstration of the Spirit and power, that your faith might not rest in the wisdom of men but in the power of God.

1 CORINTHIANS 1:17-2:5

Lectio

The context for this letter is found in verse 17. Paul was writing to the Corinthians, recalling his apostolate among them and his teaching to them, which subsequently was a source of divisions among the believers.

This letter is important because it most likely expresses a new initiative in Paul's preaching, which would explain why this particular passage is so rich in meaning. Paul describes his style of preaching in verse 17 by contrasting the wisdom of the world with the eloquence of the cross: I have not evangelized "with eloquent wisdom, lest the cross of Christ be emptied of its power." The contrast is found throughout this entire passage and is rooted in numerous contrasting senses.

Note the contrast between the vocabulary of wisdom, power, and knowledge and the vocabulary of foolishness, scandal, and weakness. While the first series of expressions describes the way in which the world acts, the second series describes the way in which God acts. This contrast is important, because in the end the meanings of these words are reversed: The foolishness of God is shown to be wiser and the weakness of God stronger than those of the world. The way in which this contrast reverses the meaning of these words is very interesting.

Of course, this excerpt is not lacking in rhetoric. But it is a type of rhetoric that has its origins in a painful experience and an amazing mystical experience. For this reason it is a very valuable text.

We find the thesis of the entire passage in verse 18: "The word of the cross is folly to those who are perishing, but to us who are being saved it is the power of God." Scriptural proof is in verses 19 and 20, where St. Paul quotes Isaiah 29:14: "Therefore, behold, I will again do marvelous things with this people, wonderful and marvelous; and the wisdom of their wise men shall perish, and the discernment of their discerning men shall be hid."

Paul wanted to emphasize the fact that Scripture had already spoken about God's working in ways that defy human wisdom. At the same time, verse 20 is referring to other passages in Isaiah that highlight the difference between the wise, gifted, and subtle debaters of this world and the way in which God acts (see Is 19:12; 33:18).

Following this scriptural confirmation for Paul's thesis, he offers us his theological reasoning in verses 21 through 24:

God has caught man unawares. When man with his human wisdom no longer knew God, God revealed himself to man through the cross—through scandal and through foolishness.

Then we come to Paul's conclusion with all its wisdom. First of all, he makes a very general statement: "For the foolishness of God is wiser than men, and the weakness of God is stronger than men." This reversal in the meaning of words has become, one might say, the law for the economy of salvation (verse 25).

Two examples follow.

The first is that of the community, found in verses 26 to 31: Paul says, in essence, "Consider your own calling, brothers. Among you there are few who are wise, powerful, or noble. You are simple, humble, and poor. You are servants, slaves, and workers. Nevertheless, God has chosen you."

This example of the community shows how God can reverse situations in the economy of salvation.

The second example, on the other hand, is the example of St. Paul himself, which is found in 1 Corinthians 2:1-5 and can be summarized, "I was with you in weakness and in much fear and trembling" (v. 3). From the Acts of the Apostles we know that Paul felt defeated after the failure of his preaching in Athens. He arrived in Corinth full of weakness, but God gave strength to his words.

Paul goes on from this reasoned conclusion in a totally different vein: "Yet among the mature we do impart wisdom,... a secret and hidden wisdom of God" (vv. 6-7). He exalts wisdom as the mystical knowledge of God's mysteries that are given to us by the Holy Spirit.

Some Ideas for Meditation

I would like to propose a meditation on this passage that can be summed up in three questions:

- What is the meaning of this text in the history of Paul's preaching and in the way in which he lived out his ministry?

- What is the meaning of this text for better understanding the situation of the Church in our times?

- What is the meaning of this text for our lives and our ministries?

Of course, through prayer and reflection on the life of St. Francis, who was pierced by the stigmata, we can truly perceive the meaning of Paul's writings. Yet perhaps the answers to these questions might also be useful.

Paul's Journey

Paul is reflecting in this passage on the way in which he preached while he was in Corinth. Therefore, we might ask him the following question: "After your failure in Athens, what did you discover at Corinth about the way in which you preached and the way in which you lived out your ministry? What became clear to you while you were in Corinth at the beginning of that winter in the year 50?"

Indeed, Paul had come to a deeper understanding of the doctrine of the cross and the consequences it had for preaching and for ministry. His many experiences as an apostle had brought him to a certain stage of maturity in the faith.

"I, too," he tells us, "preached like Peter at Pentecost at the beginning (see Acts 2) and after the healing of the crippled man (see Acts 3). I would start with the Resurrection—the glory of God that was revealed in the risen Christ—or with a divine miracle, a sign of Jesus' resurrection. I would mention Jesus' death, and yet that was not the main point of my argument. It was simply one link, though a very necessary link.

"The main point was the Resurrection, in which God showed that he was faithful to his promises. His faithfulness made up in a certain sense for the humiliating scandal of Jesus' cross; he brought justice to the injustice to which he was subjected.

"However, when I no longer had to preach to the Jews—

who needed to understand that the prophecies were fulfilled in Christ crucified and glorified—but only to the pagans, following the crises in Antioch and Pisidia (see Acts 13:46-47), I was facing a difficult decision. It's the question," Paul continues, "that each one of you needs to answer when you begin to address unbelievers or when you address the unbelief that each man harbors in his heart: Where do I begin?

"In the early days, at Lystra, for example (see Acts 14:8-18), when the pagans mistakenly took me for a god who had descended to the earth, on the spur of the moment I made up a talk on wisdom. I did not dare to speak either about the Resurrection or about the cross. I limited myself to speaking about God's plan in general.

"I developed this talk further when I was in Athens, because I wanted to find an approach that was typical of philosophical wisdom. So I talked about some unknown god, hardly mentioning the Resurrection and not even mentioning Jesus' name (see Acts 17:22-31).

"I felt bitter when my preaching to the philosophers in Athens resulted in total failure. I was compelled to reflect more deeply on the core of Christian catechesis. This was the beginning of a clear turning point in my apostolate, and it happened in Corinth. It also had some consequences for you, your life, and your preaching ministry.

"What, then, happened at Corinth? When I tried to talk to

the people, all of whom were influenced by the corruption and skepticism that you find in such a sprawling metropolis, I had an idea as to the way in which I should carry out my apostolate among the pagans. I realized that the cross is the primary and most compelling argument for converting to Christianity. This was better than an argument founded on the fear of God's imminent judgment, which John the Baptist used and I myself used when I was in Athens: 'The times of ignorance God overlooked, but now he commands all men everywhere to repent, because he has fixed a day on which he will judge the world in righteousness' (Acts 17:30-31).

"I realized, too, that the primary and most compelling argument for converting to Christianity was not an argument based on the glory of Christ, which is characterized by his resurrection from the dead and his miracles, which make it all so real, even though I have always preached on this theme. To sum it all up, I realized that the crucifixion of Jesus, the Messiah, and the Father's merciful love that was manifested through the crucifixion were the real motives for a heartfelt conversion."

At this point Paul could draw to our attention some passages from the Gospels: Zaccheus' conversion, the conversion at Simon's house of the woman who was a sinner, and the conversion of the good thief. These were conversions in which people surrendered themselves to God's incredible love.

The Prodigal Son (see Luke 15) did not experience conversion when he was overcome with hunger and decided sorrowfully and fearfully to return to his father's house. His decision was only the beginning of his conversion, the beginning of his return—what I would call a *reversion*. He experienced conversion when his father ran to meet him and hugged him. This gesture is a symbol of the triumph of the mystery of the cross and of God's incredible mercy, which the cross reveals.

In 1 Corinthians 1:17-2:5 St. Paul recalls that, as he preached in Corinth, he began to perceive with greater clarity that when people are alienated from God and are hearing the Good News for the first time, we need to let them know first and foremost about God's mercy as revealed through the mystery of the cross. We need to let them know God comes to our aid with his intimate love, a love that is paternal and maternal at the same time, in spite of our resistance. This kind of preaching fully reveals God's mercy through the atoning death of his Son on Calvary, as well as God's omnipotence, which he manifests by forgiving and saving those who were lost.

"When I was in Corinth," St. Paul goes on to say, "I noticed that the people were attentive and were surprised and overjoyed when they understood the word I was preaching. This confirmed that the cross, far from being a sign of God's weakness, is a regenerating force for believers, the basis for a solid and mature personality. Far from being foolishness, it is God's wisdom, the basis for a new knowledge of the meaning of things that is able to build a new man and a new order. I saw how even people who were uneducated or culturally deprived were able to understand the language of the cross and were being converted."

Thus, we can sum up in a few words a response to our first question. While St. Paul was evangelizing the Corinthians, he understood in a new way the divine spiritual power of the theme of the crucifixion of the Son of God, and he experienced it as a way of bringing about deep conversions among the pagans, who were also called to the faith.

The Nature of the Church Today

What does all this mean for the Church's understanding of herself in the present age? I would like to tell you about a conversation I had with a theologian, Ghislain Lafont, during a diocesan pastoral council on the nature of the Church today.

First of all, he listed some of the brightest and most vital aspects of the Church today:

- a concern for the poor that is expressed not only in almsgiving but in even more elaborate ways, to help the poor take responsibility for their own situation—to get organized and be a people and a community that are fully responsible for their fate;

- diocesan synods in which lay people participate;

- the commitment that believers have to transmit their faith;

- the birth of new communities that wish to live out the gospel in a very committed way;

- an openness to dialogue;

- the richness of contemporary theology (he noted that it is difficult to find a century in the history of the Church that is more marked by great theologians than the twentieth century);

- the presence of prophets (Martin Luther King, Jr., Bishop Oscar Romero, and Cardinal Hume among others);

- and the presence of martyrs, perhaps more than at any other time in history. (The Trappist monks who were murdered in Algeria and the many other missionaries who died for their faith come immediately to mind.)

After pointing out these bright spots, he added:

It seems to me that all these things are definitely important. At the same time, I see an importance in the humility of the different aspects of the Church. In reality, at any
given point in history, the nature of the Church cannot
be any different from Christ's nature that prevails at that
time in a Christian's consciousness.

Now, it seems to me that the image of Christ that is
predominant today is that of a servant, the Lamb of God,
the man of the beatitudes. We know in a radical way that
this aspect of humility is not only related to a need for
redemption from sins but belongs in a deeper way to
Christ's very essence.

Christian piety and theology in our time certainly
make the transition from contemplating the Sacrificed
Lamb to contemplating the Blessed Trinity. If God is
love, we cannot speak about him only in glorious and
omnipotent terms; we also need to speak about him in
terms of how he gave of himself, of how he welcomed us,
and with all the clarity that is needed when using these
terms, with words of humility and poverty.

I said something similar in my *Introductory Letter to the
Diocese,* in which I described how the Church appears today. I
looked in the Church for certain traits of Jesus—the poor
man, the humble man, the meek man, the servant who gives

his life for his brothers and sisters.[2]

This is only one way to interpret this passage from St. Paul. It is not an attempt to rationalize the Church's failures. Rather, armed with a better understanding of Christ, the Lamb who was sacrificed, it is an attempt to see within the Church the richness of his presence. This presence can help us get past the image of power and strength that the Church conveyed at certain times in its history.

Our Lives and Our Ministries

The last question touches each one of us: What does Paul's text mean for my life and my ministry?

Of course, each response will be a highly personal one. Yet the text calls us all to contemplate the mystery of the cross in prayer. Then we need to determine in light of the cross how much of his weakness God has given us the opportunity to experience. This means knowing how to look at the hardships and setbacks in life with eyes of faith. It means knowing how to look at the Church's problems and the problems we encounter in our ministry with an awareness of the fruitfulness of the cross.

This is a road that we will travel slowly—even though it is a road that we can travel quickly with words! Paul himself spent a lot of time engaged in soul-searching until he came to the full understanding that he later expressed in the First Letter to the Corinthians.

How St. Francis Taught Brother Leo That Perfect Joy Is Only in the Cross[3]

From the Little Flowers of St. Francis

One winter day St. Francis was coming to St. Mary of the Angels from Perugia with Brother Leo, and the bitter cold made them suffer keenly. St. Francis called to Brother Leo, who was walking a bit ahead of him, and he said: "Brother Leo, even if the Friars Minor in every country give a great example of holiness and integrity and good edification, nevertheless write down and note carefully that perfect joy is not in that."

And when he had walked on a bit, St. Francis called him again, saying: "Brother Leo, even if a Friar Minor gives sight to the blind, heals the paralyzed, drives out devils, gives hearing back to the deaf, makes the lame walk, and restores speech to the dumb, and what is still more, brings back to life a man who has been dead four days, write that perfect joy is not in that."

And going on a bit, St. Francis cried out again in a strong voice: "Brother Leo, if a Friar Minor knew all languages and all sciences and Scripture, if he also knew how to prophesy and to reveal not only the future but also the secrets of the consciences and minds of others, write down and note carefully that perfect joy is not in that."

And as they walked on, after a while St. Francis called again forcefully: "Brother Leo, Little Lamb of God, even if a Friar Minor could speak with the voice of an angel, and knew the courses of the stars and the powers of herbs, and knew all about the treasures in the earth, and if he knew the qualities of birds and fishes, animals, humans, roots, trees, rocks, and waters, write down and note carefully that true joy is not in that."

And going on a bit farther, St. Francis called again strongly: "Brother Leo, even if a Friar Minor could preach so well that he should convert all infidels to the faith of Christ, write down that perfect joy is not there."

Now when he had been talking this way for a distance of two miles, Brother Leo in great amazement asked him: "Father, I beg you in God's name to tell me where perfect joy is."

And St. Francis replied: "When we come to St. Mary of the Angels, soaked by the rain and frozen by the cold, all soiled with mud and suffering from hunger, and we ring at the gate of the Place and the brother porter comes and says angrily: 'Who are you?' And we say: 'We are two of your brothers.' And he contradicts us, saying: 'You are not telling the truth. Rather you are two rascals who go around deceiving people and stealing what they give to the poor. Go away!' And he does not open for us, but makes us stand outside in the snow and rain, cold and hungry, until night falls—then if we endure all those insults and cruel rebuffs patiently, without being troubled and without complaining, and if we reflect humbly and charitably that that porter really knows us and that God makes him speak against us, oh, Brother Leo, write that perfect joy is there!

"And if we continue to knock, and the porter comes out in anger, and drives us away with curses and hard blows like bothersome scoundrels, saying: 'Get away from here, you dirty thieves—go to the hospital! Who do you think you are? You certainly won't eat or sleep here!'— and if we bear it patiently and take the insults with joy and love in our hearts, oh, Brother Leo, write that that is perfect joy!

"And if later, suffering intensely from hunger and painful cold, with night falling, we still knock and call, and crying loudly beg them to open for us and let us come in for the love of God, and he grows still more angry and says: 'Those fellows are bold and shameless ruffians. I'll give them what they deserve!' And he comes out with a knotty club, and grasping us by the cowl throws us onto the ground, rolling us in the mud and snow, and beats us with that club so much that he covers our bodies with wounds—if we endure all those evils and insults and blows with joy and patience, reflecting that we must accept and bear the sufferings of the Blessed Christ patiently for love of Him, oh, Brother Leo, write: that is perfect joy!

"And now hear the conclusion, Brother Leo. Above all the graces and gifts of the Holy Spirit which Christ gives to His friends is that of conquering oneself and willingly enduring sufferings, insults, humiliations, and hardships for the love of Christ. For we cannot glory in all those other marvelous gifts of God, as they are not ours but God's, as the Apostle says: 'What have you that you have not received?'

"But we can glory in the cross of tribulations and afflictions, because that is ours, and so the Apostle says: 'I will not glory save in the Cross of Our Lord Jesus Christ!'"

To whom be honor and glory forever and ever. Amen.

"Bearing the Reproach That He Bore ... Let Us Continually Offer God a Sacrifice of Praise"

Perfect Joy in Ministry

Carlo Maria Martini

Cardinal Martini presented this meditation at the Monastery of La Verna the morning of February 17, 2000.

During the last few hours of our pilgrimage, we will ask the Lord to grant us the joy of experiencing the special grace he makes available to those who visit La Verna. We follow the example of St. Charles Borromeo, who wrote on September 3, 1579: "Today I visited La Verna, so I could take part in the devotions at this holy place, where our Savior Jesus Christ gave our glorious father, Francis, his stigmata."

During this meditation I will reflect, first of all, on the expression "perfect joy." Then I propose a *lectio* from Hebrews 13:8-15, followed by some ideas for personal meditation.

St. Francis' "Perfect Joy" and "Perfect Joy" in the Letter of James

Fr. Agostino Gemelli wrote:

> A real joy pervades all Franciscan spirituality. Note that I say joy—not merriment or gaiety (which can seem childish and noisy), nor delight (which usually does not last long because of its intensity). Joy is to merriment or gaiety what the panorama of Assisi is to the panorama of Naples.... Joy is the expression of the Franciscan concept of life.

For this reason, joy is a special grace of the Franciscan movement. Even more so, it is a special grace of La Verna, since it is here that this joy was tested in Francis' hour of darkness.

The story that is at the origin of the expression "perfect joy" is rather noteworthy. Several different accounts of it are found in various Franciscan sources. It is rooted in a command that Francis gives to Brother Leo: "Write: That is perfect joy!"

But first Francis lists the various possible reasons for perfect joy, discounting each one. If all the masters of theology in Paris or even the king of France or the king of England joined the order, Francis says, these are not reasons for perfect joy. Or if his friars were to go to the unbelievers and convert all of them to the faith, that would not be a reason for perfect joy either. That a friar would have so much grace from God that he would heal the sick is not a reason for perfect joy. What, then, is perfect joy?

I am returning from Perugia, and I am coming here at night in the dark. It is winter time and wet and muddy and so cold that icicles form at the edges of my habit and keep striking my legs, and blood flows from such wounds.

And I come to the gate, all covered with mud and cold and ice, and after I have knocked and called for a long time a friar comes and asks: "Who are you?" I answer: "Brother Francis." And he says: "Go away. This is not a decent time to be going about. You can't come in."

And when I insist again, he replies: "Go away. You are a simple and uneducated fellow. From now on don't stay with us anymore. We are so many and so important that we don't need you."

But I still stand at the gate and say: "For the love of God, let me come in tonight." And he answers: "I won't. Go to the Crosiers' Place and ask there."

I tell you that if I kept patience and was not upset—that is true joy and true virtue and the salvation of the soul.[1]

Note that when speaking about "perfect joy" (or "true joy," which are Francis' exact words), St. Francis is referring to the New Testament letter of the apostle James. For some strange reason Martin Luther did not like this letter, even though it is, as a matter of fact, intrinsic to the gospel and closely related to the Sermon on the Mount.

This is what James had to say:

Count it all joy, my brethren, when you meet various trials, for you know that the testing of your faith produces steadfastness. And let steadfastness have its full effect, that you may be perfect and complete, lacking in nothing.

James 1:2-4

Thus, Francis' words are deeply rooted in the Bible and in the Gospels. "Perfect joy" is associated with the trials that produce perseverance, and perseverance completes God's work by drawing us into the truth of Christ's salvation.

We might also recall the First Letter of Peter:

Beloved, do not be surprised at the fiery ordeal which comes upon you to prove you, as though something strange were happening to you. But rejoice in so far as you share Christ's sufferings, that you may also rejoice and be glad when his glory is revealed. If you are reproached for the name of Christ, you are blessed, because the spirit of glory and of God rests upon you.

1 Peter 4:12-14

We have to understand that early Christianity fully embraced Jesus' word, especially the last beatitude: "Blessed are you when men revile you and persecute you and utter all kinds of evil against you falsely on my account. Rejoice and be glad" (Mt 5:11-12). Thus, "perfect joy" is a grace that is found in the Gospels, a gift that God gives freely. It is a grace that he gave to St. Francis. Through the intercession of St. Francis, we can all receive this gift from the Lord.

The Text

Jesus Christ is the same yesterday and today and for ever. Do not be led away by diverse and strange teachings; for it is well that the heart be strengthened by grace, not by foods, which have not benefited their adherents. We have an altar from which those who serve the tent have no right to eat. For the bodies of those animals whose blood is brought into the sanctuary by the high priest as a sacrifice for sin are burned outside the camp. So Jesus also suffered outside the gate in order to sanctify the people through his own blood. Therefore let us go forth to him outside the camp, bearing abuse for him. For here we have no lasting city, but we seek the city which is to come. Through him then let us continually offer up a sacrifice of praise to God, that is, the fruit of lips that acknowledge his name.

HEBREWS 13:8-15

Lectio

This is the last chapter in the Letter to the Hebrews. Even though it is comprised of numerous recommendations, it has a certain unity to it. We can easily point out eight different themes:

1. The general theme is highlighted in verse 8. It was also the theme for the Holy Year of the Great Jubilee: "Jesus Christ is the same yesterday and today and for ever!"

2. An admonishment then follows in verse 9: "Do not be led away by diverse and strange teachings."

3. In verse 10 we find a rather mysterious statement regarding worship: "We have an altar from which those who serve the tent have no right to eat."

4. Verse 11 backs this statement up with a scriptural warning from Leviticus 16:27: "The bull for the sin offering and the goat for the sin offering, whose blood was brought in to make atonement in the holy place, shall be carried forth outside the camp; their skin and their flesh and their dung shall be burned with fire. "

5. Verse 12 contains the main assertion of the passage: "So Jesus also suffered outside the gate in order to sanctify the people through his own blood." Jesus, therefore, fulfilled Leviticus 16:27 by dying on the cross.

6. Verse 13 succinctly expresses the significance of Jesus' death on the cross for us: "Therefore let us go forth to him outside the camp, bearing abuse for him." It is here that we see the link between "perfect joy" in the Letter of James and Francis' understanding of perfect joy.

7. The eschatological tone of verse 14 is both interesting and significant: "For here we have no lasting city, but we seek the city which is to come."

8. Finally, verse 15 outlines the main features of Christian worship: "Through him then let us continually offer up a sacrifice of praise to God, that is, the fruit of lips that acknowledge his name."

A Closer Look

I think it good to reread some verses in this text in an effort to understand them better, keeping in mind that they are full of allusions and symbols.

The expression "Jesus is the same yesterday and today and for ever," found in verse 8, is connected with the verse that immediately precedes it: "Remember your leaders, those who spoke to you the word of God." Leaders come and go, but Christ is always with us. We need to cling to him. It is important that each one of us, and all those who are under us, learn to unite ourselves to Jesus and not to other people. Otherwise we risk losing our spiritual portion when these people are not around. Only Christ is the same yesterday, today, and forever.

Verse 9 refers to foods that do not benefit those who live by them. This is probably a reference to certain sacrifices made to idols or to certain dietary rules, but it is difficult to know exactly what the author had in mind.

Verse 10 is also a little unclear. What is the altar? We might be inclined to think that it refers to the Eucharistic table. Actually, it is the cross on which Christ was sacrificed. Through Christ's sacrifice we offer our prayers to God.

Perhaps this is to point out that the mystery of the cross, once someone accepts it, makes the Jewish sacrifices rather superfluous. As verse 12 explains, Jesus completely fulfilled the words in Leviticus by dying outside the gates of the city, or "outside the camp." For this reason a Christian's sacrifice of praise, which is a Christian life that is inspired by love, is an act of worship that is offered up to God (see verse 15).

St. Paul reflected on his own ministry: "God is my witness, whom I serve with my spirit in the gospel of his Son" (Rom 1:9). Regarding acts of charity he wrote: "I have received full payment, and more; I am filled, having received from Epaphroditus the gifts you sent, a fragrant offering, a sacrifice acceptable and pleasing to God" (Phil 4:18).

Verse 13 emphasizes the centrality of Jesus and invites us to follow him by going outside the camp, bearing the abuse—or, in other English translations, "reproach"—that he bore. This phrase is the theme of our meditation. What does it mean? What is this camp?

The Reproach

Historically "the camp" refers to a Jewish camp out in the desert. Metaphorically it refers to our comfort zone, the place where we can avoid confrontation—where we can hide behind others and not take any risks.

The Letter to the Hebrews invites us to step outside of these hidden comfort zones, which we use to protect ourselves from other people. It invites us to have the courage to leave behind these rather ordinary and mundane places, as well as everything else that prevents us from being true to ourselves and

facing up to ourselves, other people, or our day-to-day problems. This is the reason why we talk about going to Jesus on
the cross and about bearing his reproach by taking part in his
humiliation and passion.

This "reproach" or "abuse"—*oneidismon* in Greek—is also
referred to in a passage from Hebrews (11:24-26) about
Moses. This man of God "refused to be called the son of
Pharaoh's daughter, choosing rather to share ill-treatment
with the people of God than to enjoy the fleeting pleasures of
sin. He considered abuse suffered for the Christ greater wealth
than the treasures of Egypt, for he looked to the reward." Thus
Moses left behind a privileged situation that was safe and comfortable, and he made a commitment to a cause on which his
very life depended.

We can now understand better what the author meant in
Hebrews 13:13. He meant we should take courageous steps
such as Moses took in order to follow Jesus and carry his cross.

This brings to mind other important parallels in the New
Testament:

For Christ did not please himself; but, as it is written, "The
reproaches of those who reproached thee fell on me."

ROMANS 15:3

"Blessed are you when men revile you and persecute you and utter all kinds of evil against you falsely on my account. Rejoice and be glad."

Matthew 5:11-12

If you are reproached for the name of Christ, you are blessed.

1 Peter 4:14

The Greek verb *oneidizo* is always used in these passages.

At this point we can also understand more clearly the passage from Acts 5:41, where the apostles were flogged by order of the Sanhedrin. "They left the presence of the council, rejoicing that they were counted worthy to suffer dishonor for the name." St. Francis wanted this type of joy to be characteristic of his life.

Meditatio

For a time of *meditatio*, I would like to propose the following questions:

1. What reproaches of Christ are a burden for Christians?
2. What humiliations do Christians face in ministry?
3. What fosters perfect joy in ministry?

Anyone who is truly living a Christian life in today's society, where the dominant ideology is one that seeks success, pleasure, and power at any price, can feel like an outcast. Any Christian who wishes to fully follow Christ realizes sooner or later that he is living outside the mainstream. I know people who, because of their Christian beliefs, have been barred at a certain point from a career that they had all rights to pursue.

More and more, being a Christian today involves experiencing some kind of rejection. It ranges from having doors closed in our faces to slander, persecution, and even the risk of death. I have already mentioned those missionaries who have given up their lives for their faith and out of love. The list of twentieth-century martyrs—which the Holy Father himself has asked be compiled—includes thousands and thousands of names.

What does it mean to experience "perfect joy" in such situations? It is not an easy thing to explain, insofar as this joy is a gift from God. It is a grace that comes from the Holy Spirit to demonstrate the triumph of the risen Jesus over our human condition, now that we have been joined to Christ.

One of the people who remind me most of this extraordinary grace of "perfect joy" is Cardinal Joseph Bernardin, who died of cancer on November 14, 1996. In his book *The Gift of Peace*, he described the last three years of his life. I would like to quote a couple of passages:

The past three years have taught me a great deal about myself and my relationship to God, the Church, and others. Three major events within these years have led me to where I am today. First, the false accusation of sexual misconduct in November 1993 and my eventual reconciliation with my accuser a year later. Second, the diagnosis of pancreatic cancer in June 1995 and the surgery that rendered me "cancer free" for fifteen months. And third, the cancer's return at the end of August 1996, this time in the liver, and my decision to discontinue chemotherapy one month later and live the rest of my life as fully as possible.[2]

During this latter period Cardinal Bernardin devoted himself in a special way to comforting cancer victims. He visited many and corresponded with others. In his book he characterized these three years as "years that have been as joyful as they have been difficult":

To paraphrase Charles Dickens in *A Tale of Two Cities*, "it has been the best of times, it has been the worst of times." The *worst* because of the humiliation, physical pain, anxiety and fear. The *best* because of the reconciliation, love, pastoral sensitivity and peace that have resulted from God's grace and the support and prayers of so many people.[3]

Cardinal Bernardin's reflections help us understand this grace of "joy" that we find in the Gospels. This is a grace that we cannot presume to have but that the Lord gives freely to whoever asks for it and admires his saints for it.

Humiliations in Ministry

There are many ways in which we can experience the humiliations in our ministry that Christ experienced in his ministry. You probably experience them more than I do. Nevertheless, I would like to recall some of them.

Realizing that we priests are a minority within society, we need to live out our commitment without complaining and without feeling bad. The grace of the Spirit helps us to understand that this in itself requires great effort on our part and is a form of humiliation. But at the same time, it is an opportunity for us to exercise greater pastoral care.

Another form of humiliation in ministry is feeling "out of it," because we are "out of sync" with the rhythm of the pleasures and rewards of the contemporary world.

It is also part of Christ's shame to be rejected or to be subjected to personal attacks.

During a time of silence we can profitably analyze situations in which we participate in Christ's shame. This will help us understand how the Lord is inviting us to experience them with his grace.

I would like to cite the example of Fr. Vincenzo Arrigoni, one of our priests, who died on June 20, 1998. Two months before he died, I made a pastoral visit to his parish. Even though he was already seriously ill with a terminal illness, he continued to carry on his ministry out of the sheer strength of his will and with admirable courage.

Such an illness can be a source of humiliation. He left behind a beautiful testimony of "perfect joy" during such a time:

May your will be done! But what the Lord wants is our happiness. God always wants good, and he transforms everything into good! In spite of everything that might happen to us, God wants good for us! It might happen that in the world no one wishes good for us, but God wants good for us, and this is sufficient reason to be good!

What Fosters Perfect Joy?

Finally, let us reflect briefly on what fosters "perfect joy." How can we get this attitude deeply rooted in our hearts?

We already know that it is a gift. The passages from Cardinal Bernardin's book show us the difficulties that he had to endure. We recall the serious charges of sexual abuse that were so widely reported throughout the United States. His reputation was tarnished because of this slander. He had to muster all his energy in order to win the battle and be exonerated. Moreover, he reconciled with the person who had made the accusations against him.

"Perfect joy" is a part of the gift of faith and hope. The Lord calls us to pray unceasingly, "Lord, increase our faith and our hope!"

Along with faith and with prayer, the support of other people is very important. In our participation in Christ's humiliation, we become aware of the fact—thanks to God—that there are people who support us by interceding for us. As Cardinal Bernardin reminds us:

For me, this moment of public accusation and inquiry was also a moment of grace. A moment of pain, but a moment of grace because I felt the great love and support that many people were giving me.[4]

And about the difficult test of his illness he wrote:

In these dark moments, besides my faith and trust in the Lord, I was constantly bolstered by the awareness that thousands of people were praying for me throughout the Archdiocese and, indeed, the world. I have been graced by an outpouring of affection and support that has allowed me to experience ecclesial life as a "community of hope" in a very intimate way.[5]

This is the great gift of the communion of saints—of those who are already with God and of all those who are traveling with us the path of this world.

Let us experience these last hours of our pilgrimage in silence, in recollection and in reflection, thanking God for the presence of the saints in our lives and for the support we receive from other people in our battle of faith.

"Beauty and Crucified Love": Ministry and Conforming to Christ Crucified

Final Thoughts

Marco Bove

Marco Bove is a director of the Istituto sacerdotale Maria Immacolata in Milan, Italy.

There is no doubt that Francis' experience of faith was rich and well articulated. Francis was a man of his times, part of the contradictions and tensions that characterized the ordinary people and merchants of Italy in the thirteenth century. At the same time, he was able to interpret the deep spiritual aspirations of his time.

Francis is also a man of our times. He is able to address the fears and expectations of the many men and women today whose lives are characterized by fatigue and disillusionment. These people are searching for something that truly can give them faith and hope amid the passing days and the multiple projects of life.

Living out our ministry today, proclaiming the good news

of the cross and the beauty of crucified Love, and letting the stories from Francis' life speak to us: These endeavors are very challenging and yet very relevant for our own faith experience.

Let us examine more closely two events in Francis' journey that are very symbolic: receiving the gift of the stigmata at La Verna and composing the "Canticle of the Creatures" toward the end of his life.

Following Jesus, Who Is Poor and Crucified

The gift that Francis received at La Verna was above all a visible and *definitive* expression of the tension by which he was guided: the desire to follow Jesus and the desire to conform his life to Jesus, poor and crucified. The signs of the passion that he bore on his body were a visible expression of this deep aspiration.

Francis basically remained a *poor man*, a man who lived by faith and who gave his life totally to God. Such a man does not make calculated plans and does not seek security in what he has, who he is, or what he knows. The Father is the source for everything, and the poor man places his trust completely in God.

One does not maintain such an inner attitude without a struggle and without intense suffering. When Francis arrived at La Verna, he was full of many doubts: about himself, the trail he was blazing, the order he had founded, the choices he had made, the future, and his responsibility in regards to all this.

Now, Francis did not just find himself in such a state of abandonment; he welcomed it and embraced it as a gift of grace. He had reached a point of complete trust, such that he could be before God and before himself *as a poor man.*

Like Jesus, Francis also sought the Father's will. Gradually God led him to the total gift of himself, to the experience of the cross: "My Father,... not as I will, but as thou wilt" (Mt 26:39). Herein lies the meaning of the stigmata. It is the external manifestation of something that occurred in the heart, so as to enable Francis to say with St. Paul, "It is no longer I who live, but Christ who lives in me" (Gal 2:20).

The inner struggle leading up to total surrender often assumes a form of *resistance* in the life of the believer. In opposition to the weakness and the foolishness of the cross are the wisdom and power of this world, which are rooted in a quest for clarity and efficiency based on expediency. But Jesus' cross is not based on any human criteria, and even less on any criteria related to expediency, efficiency, or effectiveness, because God's strength and wisdom are revealed through Jesus' cross.

Therefore, we might ask ourselves the following questions about our ministry in the light of the life of this man who was poor and crucified:

- What does it mean to live out my ministry as one who is *poor?* Do I seek strength and security in what I have, what I know, and who I am? What signs of poverty—not only symbolic signs but concrete signs as well—do I see in my own life? What signs are lacking?

- The opposite of trust is a sort of restless tension in our lives that causes excessive unrest, anxiety, and fear. Do I experience this at times? When?

- Do I seek God's will for my life and the lives of those under my care, both as a sign of self-deprivation and of self-renunciation? Where is the *cross* in my ministry?

- What kinds of resistance and what *worldly* logic do I see in myself most frequently? A preoccupation with numbers? A longing to be successful? A search for approval? A lack of attention to the needs of others?

Singing About the Beauty of God

The second event from the life of Francis that we examine more closely is the "Canticle of the Creatures." Francis was a man who *learned* to *sing.* His life was first and foremost an expression of genuine *joy*, not sentimentalism or idealization.

Francis defined this joy as "perfect joy."

What is perfect joy? What is at its root?

Looking at Francis' life and writings, we can say that it is a deep inner peace. This gift enabled him to remain peaceful and, whenever necessary, to *find that peace once again* in the Spirit. This was true even during difficult moments when fear or rebellion was a temptation.

This, then, is "joy" according to Francis. This is the profound meaning of Christian joy. It is not rooted in an absence of difficulties or worries. And we cannot attain it by trying to create the conditions needed to remain peaceful. Rather, it is a fruit of the gift of God, the ability to enter into everything certain of God's love and provision for us. The experience of joy and peace is, first and foremost, a profound experience of faith, the gift of superabundant grace.

But if joy is an interior state that characterizes the heart of a person who has been visited by grace, we might now ask, What was the peak point for Francis? What was his experience of faith, which is the fruit of an encounter with God? What was the *outcome* of La Verna?

Leaving La Verna, Francis went immediately to Umbria and the Marches on a long preaching tour. His biographers say that he was deeply inspired and very enthusiastic. Was this, then, the outcome?

In the "Canticle of the Creatures," Francis expresses what

might be the key to his journey of faith: *praise* and *gratitude*. This text is not some testimony to a certain *season* in his life, such as his approaching end. Nor is it just a very beautiful hymn of praise. Above all, it expresses a *way of life*, an inner attitude in which Francis learned to stand before the Father and to face life itself. Praise bursts forth from the heart of a man who lives by grace and by grace alone, from the heart of a man who can only express *gratitude* through his life and through his words.

As one last catalyst for meditation, I pose some questions on faith and joy in regard to our ministry:

- Am I happy to be a priest? Does it show? Can I say that I am in a position to find peace in the Spirit and rise up above the difficulties, fatigue, and disillusionments that are inevitable?

- Am I capable of gratitude? Or is everything a duty or something that I take for granted? Do I know how to recognize the good that comes not only from the Lord but also from the many simple people whom I have the opportunity to meet?

- Is my prayer capable of praise and *song?* Would I be able to compose my own "Canticle"?

- The opposite of praise and gratitude is complaining. Do I find that at times I have the tendency to criticize too freely and too easily? Do I habitually look down on others? Do I suffer from *chronic* dissatisfaction? How do I respond to all this?

- What joy and what enthusiasm do I recognize in the words I preach, in the teachings I give, and in my simple conversations with people?

Like Francis, we, too, can adopt gratitude as a spiritual attitude to interpret our entire ministry: the way in which we confront problems, where our heart is as we carry out our responsibilities, and the discretion we apply to every relationship.

Every proclamation of the Good News and all genuine preaching can only originate here, in this superabundance that we find in our hearts, in this uncontainable praise. This song of life manifests the beautiful, enchanting, and desirable face of a God to whom we can entrust our entire lives.

At the root of the proclamation of the gospel and of every *mission*, therefore, there is a very deep experience of faith and joy. Only praise and gratitude in the heart of an apostle can produce the *right* words and the *right* emphasis to speak to the hearts of people and reveal to them a beauty that is truly *incomparable*.

~Notes ~

Chapter One
The Lord Has "Put a New Song in My Mouth, a Song of Praise to Our God"

1. "The Prayer *Absorbeat,*" quoted from Marion A. Habig, ed., *St. Francis of Assisi, Writings and Early Biographies: English Omnibus of Sources for the Life of St. Francis* (Chicago: Franciscan Herald, 1983), 161.
2. "The Testament of St. Francis" (1226), Habig, 68.
3. Carlo Maria Martini, *Quale bellezza salverà il mondo? Lettera pastorale 1999-2000*, 31.
4. St. Francis of Assisi, "Praises of God," Habig, 125-26.
5. St. Francis of Assisi, "The Canticle of Brother Sun," Habig, 130-31.

Chapter Two
"All Praise Be Yours, My Lord, Through All That You Have Made"

1. Habig, 1020.
2. Habig, 1021.
3. Paul Claudel, *The Tidings Brought to Mary*, Act IV, Scene 3.

4. St. Augustine, *The Confessions of St. Augustine*, XI, 14 (17), John K. Ryan, trans. (Garden City, N.Y.: Image, 1960), 287.

5. Paul Claudel, *The Satin Slipper*, Act III, Scene 8.

6. Feodor Dostoevski, *The Idiot*, Part III, Chapter 5.

7. Arthur Rimbaud, *Sister of Charity*.

8. Charles Baudelaire, *The Vampire*.

9. Serge Bulgakov as quoted by Paul Evdokimov in *The Art of the Icon: the Theology of Beauty* (Oakwood Publications, Redondo Beach, Calif., 1990), 88.

10. Evdokimov, 37-38.

11. Giovanni Pico della Mirandola, *On the Dignity of Man* (New York: Bobbs-Merrill, 1965), 5.

12. *Confessions*, X, 27 (38), 254.

13. See Irenaeus, *Adversus haereses*, V, 16, 2; *Demonstrations* 22.

14. See Augustine, *Retractions*, I, 1.

15. Feodor Dostoevski, *Lettera all nipote Sonja Ivanova*, in *L'Idiota* (Garzanti, Milan, 1983), XII.

16. Paul Claudel, *The Humiliation of the Father*, Act 1, Scene 1.

17. St. John Climacus, Colm Luibheid, trans. *The Ladder of Divine Ascent*, XV, 105 (Ramsey, N.J.: Paulist, 1982), 179.

18. Tertullian, *De cultu foeminarum*.

19. Augustine, *Confessions*, X, 34, (53), 264.

20. St. John Climacus, *The Ladder of Divine Ascent,* XV, 98, 160.

21. St. Thomas Aquinas, *Summa theologiae,* I-IIae, q. 109, a 1, ad 1.

22. Johann Wolfgang von Goethe, *Faust,* Close of Part II.

23. Martin Luther, *Sermoni sui Vangeli,* ed. Weimar, X, I, 68.

24. "The Testament of St. Francis," Habig, 67-70.

Chapter Three
"This Is My Testament"

1. "The Testament of St. Francis," Habig, 69.

2. Dante Alighieri, *Paradise,* XI, 106 s.

3. "The Testament of St. Francis," Habig, 67.

4. Tommaso da Celano, "Second Life," II, 6, Habig, 365-66.

5 Tommaso da Celano, "First Life," VII, 17, Habig, 242-43.

6. "The Testament of St. Francis," Habig, 67.

7. See B. Cornet, *Le "De reverential corporis Christi," Exhortation et lettres de Saint François,* in "Etudes Franciscaines," LVIII (1956), 155-71.

8. "The Legend of Perugia," 115, Habig, 1089.

9. "The Testament of St. Francis," Habig, 67.

10. See Cornet, 157-62.

11. St. Francis of Assisi, "Letter to All Clerics," Habig, 100-101.

12. See Hefele, Conciles, 1348-50, quoted in Cornet, 162.

13. St. Leo the Great, *Second Discourse on the Ascension*, 2.

14. Tommaso da Celano, XXX, 84, Habig, 299.

15. Francis of Assisi, "Letter to a General Chapter," Habig, 105-106.

16. "The Testament of St. Francis," Habig, 67-68.

17. "Letter to All the Faithful," Habig, 93.

18. "Letter to a General Chapter," Habig, 107.

19. "The Testament of St. Francis," Habig, 68.

20. See "Legend of the Three Companions," 29, Habig, 917-18.

21. Celano, "First Life," IX, 22, 246-47 and "Second Life," X, 15, Habig, 374-75).

22. Celano, "First Life," IX, 22, Habig, 247.

23. "The Testament of St. Francis," Habig, 68.

24. St. Bonaventure, "Major Life of St. Francis," VII, Habig, 680-88.

25. Dante Alighieri, 112-14.

26. Bonaventure, VII, 1 and 6, Habig, 680, 684.

27. St. Francis of Assisi, "Rule of 1223," X, Habig, 63.

28. "The Testament of St. Francis," Habig, 70.

29. Translated from *Fonti Francescane* (Padua, Italy: Edizioni Messaggero, 1980), paragraphs 829-31, pages 740-42.

Chapter Four
Man's Wisdom and Power, God's Weakness and Foolishness

1. Carlo Maria Martini, *Parlo al tuo cuore. Per una regola di vita del cristiano ambrosiano, Lettera pastorale per l'anno 1996-1997* (Milan: Centro ambrosiano, 1996), 18, n. 8.
2. See Carlo Maria Martini, "Lettera di presentazione alla diocesi," Diocesi di Milano, Sinodo 47, (Milan: Centro ambrosiano, 1995), 15-46, n. 6; 20-23.
3. "The Little Flowers of St. Francis," Habig, 1318-20.

Chapter Five
*"Bearing the Reproach That He Bore …
Let Us Continually Offer God a Sacrifice of Praise"*

1. "The Perfect Joy," Habig, 1501-2; see also "Little Flowers of St. Francis," VIII, Habig, 1318-20.
2. Joseph Cardinal Bernardin, *The Gift of Peace* (Chicago: Loyola, 1997), 10-11.
3. Bernardin, ix.
4. Bernardin, 28.
5. Bernardin, 109-10.